AI in Law: Justice by Algorithm

GoodMan, Volume 1

Patrick Mukosha

Published by Patrick Mukosha, 2025.

Also by Patrick Mukosha

GoodMan

Resilient Strategies: Thriving in Harsh Business Conditions
Strategic Entrepreneurship: Navigating The Path To Success
Decisive Power: Navigating How to Make Toughest Decisions
"Reigning the Boardroom: A Trailblazing Guide to Corporate Governance Success"
Fortifying Digital Fortress: A Comprehensive Guide to Information Systems Security
"Unleashing the Power of Inclusive Innovation: Transforming the World for All"
"Exploring Computer Systems: From Fundamentals to Advanced Concepts"
"Computer Viruses Unveiled: Types, Trends and Mitigation Strategies"
"The Pinnacle of Success: Unveiling the World's 20 Most Successful Brands in 2023"
"Mastering Relational Databases: From Fundamentals to Advanced Concepts"
"Navigating Change: A Comprehensive Guide to Change Management"
"Information Systems Unraveled: Exploring the Core Concepts"
"Careers in Information Technology: Network Engineer"

“Careers in Information Technology: Network and Systems Administrator”
“Careers in Information Technology: Database Administrator”
"Careers in Information Technology: Cybersecurity Analyst"
“Careers in Information Technology: Cloud Security Specialist”
"Careers in Information Technology: Blockchain Developer"
"Careers in Information Technology: DevOps Engineer"
"Careers in Information Technology: Quality Assurance Analyst"
"Careers in Information Technology: Machine Learning Engineer"
"Careers in Information Technology: Artificial Intelligence (AI) Engineer"
"Careers in Information Technology: Internet of Things (IoT) Developer"
"Careers in Information Technology: AR/VR Developer"
“Careers in Information Technology: IoT Embedded Systems Designer”
“Careers in Information Technology: Artificial Intelligence (AI) Robotics Engineer”
“Careers in Information Technology: IoT Solutions Engineer”
“Careers in Information Technology: Data Scientist”
"Careers in Information Technology: Computer Vision Engineer"
"The Sociology of Information Technology"
“Smart Cities: The Technology Transforming Urban Living”
"The Future of Connectivity: Unleashing the Power of 5G and Beyond"
" Cybersecurity 2030 - Strategies for a Secure Digital Future"
The AI-Human Merger: Becoming Super-Intelligent Beings
AI Unleashed: The Future of Artificial Intelligence and Human Evolution
The Digital Prophet: Predicting the Next Decade of Disruption
AI in Agriculture: Farming the Future
AI in Education: Teaching the Machines to Teach

Deep Signal: AI and IoT Unlocking Underground Mining Communication

AI in Energy: Powering the Smart Grid

The Great Unlearning: How Artificial Intelligence Is Rewriting the Value of a Degree

AI in Law: Justice by Algorithm

AI in Law: Justice by Algorithm

Legal Research Automation, Contract Analysis, Predictive Judgments, and AI in Courtrooms.

In the legal field, Artificial Intelligence (AI) refers to the use of machine learning and algorithms to carry out tasks like document review, legal research, and data management that are typically completed by legal professionals. It is an important subfield in legal technology, sometimes referred to as legal informatics. – Patrick Mukosha

Copyright Notice

First Published: November, 2025

Publisher: Dr. Patrick Mukosha

Trademarks

All terms mentioned in this book that are known to be trademarks or service marks have been appropriately capitalized. The Author and the publisher cannot attest to the accuracy of this information. Use of a term in this book should not be regarded as affecting the validity of any trademark or service mark.

Warning and Disclaimer

Every effort has been made to make this book as complete and as accurate as possible, but no warranty or fitness is implied. The information provided in this book is on as is basis. The Author and the Publisher shall have neither liability nor responsibility to any person or entity with respect to any loss or damage arising from the use the information contained in this book.

Author: Dr. Patrick Mukosha

Abstract

AI in Law: ***Justice by Algorithm*** investigates how *Artificial Intelligence* can revolutionize contemporary legal practice. This *book offers a thorough road map of AI's effects on law, ethics, and justice, from automating contract analysis and legal research to predictive judgments and AI-assisted courtrooms.*

Patrick Mukosha highlights the indispensable role of human judgment, ethics, and accountability while illustrating how AI can improve efficiency, lessen bias, and increase access to justice through global case studies, from COMPAS risk assessments in the US to China's Smart Courts and Singapore's integrated AI platforms.

Readers will learn:

- *How AI is changing litigation strategy, legal research, and drafting;*
- *Predictive tools that support attorneys and judges without taking the place of discretion;*
- *The future of law as a cooperative human-AI ecosystem that combines professional knowledge with technology insight;*
- *Ethical and regulatory frameworks guaranteeing justice, openness, and privacy.*

This book is a comprehensive guide to comprehending, applying, and regulating AI in the pursuit of justice, making it perfect for legal professionals, students, legislators, and anybody interested in the nexus of law, technology, and society.

Enter the "Justice by Algorithm" era, where artificial intelligence and human judgment combine to create the laws of the future.

Chapter 1: The Dawn of Digital Justice

This chapter examines how legal practice has changed over time, emphasizing the advent of digital tools and the first uses of artificial intelligence in legal study. The early use of AI in document inspection and precedent analysis is demonstrated through case studies.

1.1. The Law and Technology Convergence

The law has developed slowly for centuries. The courtroom remained a temple of tradition, its customs unaltered, its volumes brimming with precedent, even while technology revolutionized communication, transportation, and business. However, the hitherto distinct domains of silicon and statute started to blend together as artificial intelligence became widely used in the twenty-first century.

One of the most significant developments in legal history is *the rise of digital justice*, a court system enhanced by algorithms, data analytics, and machine reasoning.

Beyond just digitizing paper, *the digital revolution has completely changed how justice is perceived, administered, and experienced.* AI can now evaluate contracts in a matter of seconds, make remarkably accurate predictions about court decisions, and even help form legal opinions.

What started out as an efficiency experiment has developed into a rethinking of the rule of law?

1.2. A Synopsis of Legal Innovation from Quills to Quantum

Its instruments have always been reflected in the legislation. Gutenberg's printing press democratized legal documents in the fifteenth century, making statutes and precedents more widely accessible. When the typewriter was invented in the late 19th century, legal drafting became more standardized. *Case law retrieval became quick with the advent of electronic legal databases such as Westlaw and LexisNexis during the 1980s computer revolution.*

The internet then emerged, bringing in e-justice through electronic discovery, virtual hearings, and online filings. This shift was expedited by the COVID-19 outbreak, which demonstrated that justice could be served even when judges, attorneys, and plaintiffs were located on other continents. But these were only forerunners. Artificial intelligence is a leap from digitization to cognition rather than the next stage.

1.3. Initial Digital Justice Case Studies

Case Study 1: The US COMPAS Scandal

AI gained international legal attention in 2016 with the State v. Loomis case. Eric Loomis contested his sentence, claiming that his right to due process was violated by the COMPAS (*Correctional Offender Management Profiling for Alternative Sanctions)* algorithm used to determine his likelihood of reoffending.

Although the algorithm had a significant impact on his punishment, both the defense and the court were unaware of its proprietary and opaque rationale.

The Wisconsin Supreme Court maintained COMPAS's usage, but the case sparked a global discussion about algorithmic fairness, prejudice, and transparency.

If justice's logic was hidden in a "black box," could it really be impartial?

The conversation around AI ethics in law is still shaped by this question.

Case Study 2: Predictive Policing in the Netherlands and the United Kingdom

Data-driven models were utilized in initiatives like the Dutch Crime Anticipation System (CAS) and the UK's PredPol to forecast crime hotspots. Critics claimed they perpetuated systematic bias by forecasting more crime in vulnerable neighbourhoods just because there was already more enforcement there, despite the fact that they demonstrated some success in allocating resources.

These early lessons showed that, rather than eliminating inequality, data without context might exacerbate it.

Case Study 3: The Smart Courts Initiative in Singapore

When it comes to digital transformation, Singapore's judiciary has been a global leader. Court procedures have been expedited by its Integrated Electronic Litigation System and experimental use of AI for case triage and legal research. *Online Dispute Resolution* (ODR) platforms have significantly decreased case backlogs, and judges now receive AI-generated summaries to aid in deliberation. This is how digital justice works in tandem with human judgment rather than in its place.

1.4. The New Legal Transformation Pillars

Three fundamental foundations support the emergence of AI in law:

1.4.1. **Automation of Routine Tasks:**

AI systems like ROSS Intelligence and Kira Systems now handle legal research, document review, and contract analysis, significantly reducing expenses and turnaround times. Junior associates may now finish tasks that used to take weeks in a matter of minutes, freeing up human lawyers to engage in more sophisticated reasoning.

1.4.2. **Predictive Analytics and Legal Forecasting:**

Algorithms can accurately forecast litigation outcomes by examining thousands of previous cases. Businesses like Lex Machina and Premonition assert that they can determine which attorney does the best before which judge, turning litigation strategy into a data science.

1.4.3. **Ethical and Judicial Augmentation:**

AI is improving judgment rather than only taking the place of labour. The concept of impartiality is being redefined by tools that find anomalies in case law, suggest equitable precedents, and uncover prejudice in sentencing.

1.5. Notable Turning Points: The 2018 Toronto AI Court Pilot

When Algorithms Met the Law an AI system that suggested outcomes in insurance disputes was tested by a minor civil claims court in Ontario. A 92% concordance rate was discovered when human judges compared their rulings with the AI's output. The exercise demonstrated AI's potential as a consistency engine rather than undermining human authority:

- **Estonia's "Robot Judge" Project (2020):**

For minor claims under €7,000, the Estonian government revealed plans for an AI-based adjudicator. Preliminary decisions made by the AI could be appealed to a human judge. This effort showed how tiny countries may lead in judicial innovation, even though it is still in its early stages.

- **China's "Smart Court"**

Incorporates facial recognition, blockchain evidence authentication, and automated judgment drafting, has processed over 100 million cases using its AI-powered judicial platform. The model shows how AI can handle enormous caseloads in intricate legal ecosystems, despite ongoing worries about state control.

1.6. Ethical Crossroads: Digital Justice's Human Factor

Can algorithms administer justice without empathy?

This conundrum is at the heart of digital justice. AI is exceptionally consistent, but it lacks moral intuition—the human sensitivity to situation, regret, and change. For instance, the Loomis case raised important concerns about whether data-driven decisions could ever completely comprehend the human condition that led to the crime.

Academics caution against the emergence of "technocratic justice," in which *data efficiency takes precedence over moral consideration*. On the other hand, some contend that AI presents an opportunity to address centuries of human prejudice.

Instead of replacing judges, the solution is to redefine their collaboration with technology so that human empathy and computer accuracy coexist.

1.7. Law without Lawyers

AI's democratization of legal information also poses grave concerns for the legal profession.

What function does a lawyer still play if machines are able to design contracts, forecast case outcomes, and provide legal advice?

In the future, some see lawyers as "AI conductors," directing, auditing, and interpreting algorithmic results instead of conducting research and drafting by hand.

- *Legal education needs to change as well.*
    - *Future attorneys will need to comprehend algorithms and data ethics in addition to laws and precedents. Law schools will produce hybrid practitioners that are proficient in both computational logic and jurisprudence.*

1.8. The Path Ahead

A new legal era is about to begin. In the same way that the Industrial Revolution changed the nature of labour, *the AI revolution is changing the legal profession by making practitioners re-evaluate both the definition of justice and how it is administered.* Even though the courtroom of the future will be virtual, its core values—fairness, honesty, and accountability—will remain human.

The emergence of *digital justice* is a reawakening of our shared quest for equity—*enhanced, expedited, and illuminated by artificial intelligence*—rather than a capitulation to machines.

Chapter 2: Automation of Legal Research and the Emergence of Cognitive Law Assistants

This chapter investigates the effects of AI-powered legal research tools on accuracy, efficiency, and precedent access. Provides practical instances of enhanced case preparation using platforms like as Westlaw Edge and ROSS Intelligence.

2.1. The Legal Knowledge Burden

Fundamentally, *law is a discipline of precedent.* Every ruling builds on the framework of its predecessors, creating an intricate web of logic that spans generations. However, as this web grows, it becomes almost difficult for any human mind to fully comprehend it. By the early 2000s, thousands of new rulings, regulations, and commentary were introduced daily across international jurisdictions, overwhelming legal practitioners with data.

Despite their thoroughness, traditional legal research methodologies were becoming outdated. Before keyword-based search engines took their place, lawyers had to spend endless hours poring over dusty law papers, which only slightly reduced the workload. Comprehension—machines that could comprehend the law rather than merely retrieve it—was what was lacking.

AI developed to close that gap.

2.2. From Searching for Keywords to Understanding Semantics

Access to legal information was transformed by the first wave of digital legal tools, including Westlaw and LexisNexis. However, Boolean search logic—which is exact but strict—was the main method used by these systems. A crucial precedent could be overlooked if a term is overlooked.

The use of Natural Language Processing (NLP), *which enables computers to understand human language in context,* was the breakthrough. This made it possible for legal AI systems to understand meaning, subtlety, and relevance in addition to precise language.

ROSS Intelligence, which debuted in 2015 and was based on IBM's Watson, is a notable example. Promoted as "the world's first AI lawyer," ROSS was capable of answering natural language questions such as *"What is the standard for establishing negligence in a medical malpractice case in California?"* It scanned millions of documents in a matter of seconds and produced a condensed legal response with supporting documentation.

A paradigm change from searching the law to understanding it was highlighted by the success of ROSS Intelligence.

Case Study: The Artificial Intelligence that Outwitted the Associate

> 20 seasoned corporate attorneys were compared to an AI system trained for contract assessment in a 2018 LawGeex study. Both were entrusted with detecting vulnerabilities in Non-Disclosure Agreements (NDAs). The human attorneys finished the work in 92 minutes with an average accuracy of 85%. In just 26 seconds, the AI achieved 94% accuracy. This investigation highlighted an important fact: machines

were starting to match human analytical precision in well specified legal tasks, not just being faster.

For junior associates whose billable hours previously relied on laborious research, this posed an existential danger, while others praised it as a release from tedium. The true revolution, however, was more subtle: the lawyer's function was changing from information retrieval to strategic interpretation.

2.3. The New Workflow and Cognitive Law Assistants

The next phase of development, known as cognitive law assistants, is represented by contemporary AI research platforms like *Westlaw Edge, Lex Machina, and Casetext's CoCounsel.* These systems combine deep learning, NLP, and predictive analytics to deliver contextual insights instead of unprocessed data.

For instance, using OpenAI's GPT technology, Casetext CoCounsel can do tasks like creating discovery requests, summarizing depositions, and composing notes in a matter of seconds:

- *Lex Machina*, created at Stanford, employs data analytics to identify trends in judicial behaviour, assisting attorneys in forecasting the decisions that particular judges may make in patent or securities cases.
- To lower the danger of citing out-of-date law, Westlaw Edge uses AI-driven KeyCite Overruling danger to alert users when a case may have been compromised by subsequent rulings.

By increasing the lawyer's cognitive ability and facilitating more strategic decision-making, these tools serve as enhanced partners rather than replacements.

2.4. Human-Machine Collaboration in the Legal System

Legal firms are no longer the only ones using AI in legal research. To help in decision-making, courts themselves are starting to use cognitive technologies. While the Supreme People's Court in China runs an AI-powered "Smart Court" platform that retrieves pertinent legal texts, suggests precedents, and even drafts preliminary opinions for human judges to review, the HM Courts & Tribunals Service in the UK uses digital platforms to expedite case management.

One noteworthy case study is from Shanghai, where prosecutors were aided by the introduction of the "206 System." In order to give suggestions that are not legally binding, the system examines the evidence, legal rules, and sentencing guidelines.

It has been credited with lowering human mistake and fostering consistency in more than 100,000 cases, but detractors warn that if it is applied without supervision, it might undermine judicial discretion.

2.5. The Singularity of Legal Research When Results Are Predicted by Data

AI algorithms that have been educated on enormous case law libraries are anticipating judicial behaviour in addition to retrieving precedents. Predictive analytics can forecast the likelihood that a lawsuit will be successful, the length of a trial, or even the inclinations of specific judges.

An algorithm that accurately predicted 79% of results in cases before the European Court of Human Rights was created in 2016 by researchers at University College London and the University of Sheffield. Litigation finance firms utilize similar approaches to evaluate investment potential and risk, turning case law into quantitative data.

The ramifications are profound: *law, which was formerly thought to be an art of persuasion, is now a science of probability.*

2.6. Epistemic and Ethical Difficulties

Although there is no denying AI's effectiveness in legal research, there are significant epistemic hazards associated with it. Algorithms that have been trained on past decisions may unintentionally replicate systemic biases, reflecting historical injustices rather than the goals of justice.

Furthermore, the opacity of machine reasoning—often referred to as the "black box problem"—raises questions regarding accountability and transparency in judicial decision-making:

- *The algorithm that locates your precedent is audited by whom?*
- *Who makes sure that the machine's interpretation of "relevance" complies with due process and fairness standards?*

The need for *Explainable AI* (XAI) in law is becoming more pressing as legal systems depend more and more on insights produced by AI. In high-risk areas like justice, regulatory frameworks like the OECD AI Principles and the EU's Artificial Intelligence Act (2024) increasingly place a strong emphasis on human monitoring, traceability, and openness.

2.7. Legal Education's Comeback

Legal education is changing as a result of the evolution of legal research. Computational law, data analytics, and AI ethics are being taught in law schools all around the world. In order to successfully query AI systems, check their results, and comprehend algorithmic limits, students are taught to work with machines.

The modern lawyer is a legal technologist, proficient in both digital thinking and jurisprudence, rather than just a researcher.

Prominent organizations like Harvard's Berkman Klein Centre for Internet & Society and Stanford's CodeX (Centre for Legal Informatics) are leading the way in multidisciplinary studies that combine computer science with law. The next generation of legal scholars will be just as at ease deciphering algorithms as they are evaluating statutes.

2.8. Towards Algorithmic Integrity

The integrity of algorithmic systems becomes critical as the era of digital justice deepens. *Algorithmic law requires computational fairness, a criterion that guarantees the datasets, parameters, and logic behind AI systems reflect equitable principles, just as traditional law necessitates procedural fairness.*

AI auditability and ethical certification for legal tech solutions are currently being demanded by international bar groups and judicial councils. The goal is clear: AI must strengthen the legitimacy of justice rather than undermine it.

2.9. The Cognitive Renaissance of Law in Conclusion

The emergence of *Cognitive Law Assistants* signifies a revival of legal research rather than its demise. Although machines can now read the law more quickly, remember it perfectly, and even predict its course, they are still unable to comprehend justice in the moral sense. In order to ensure that the warmth of human judgment is never replaced by the frigid precision of code, the human lawyer continues to serve as the translator of conscience.

Contract analysis and smart legal agreements represent the next frontier, where algorithms will not only identify the law but also carry it out.

Autonomous legislation is emerging in the era of cognitive science.

Chapter 3: Contract Analysis: The Era of Intelligent Legal Contracts

3.1. The Contract: The Algorithm of Civilization

Contracts were the first algorithms created by humans long before computers. They were collections of conditional instructions that dictated what would happen when certain requirements were fulfilled. *"I will cover the cost if you deliver the goods."* The aim was binding, and the reasoning was binary. However, as economies expanded and transactions became more international, contracts became increasingly complicated and essential to both trade and governance.

Relationships with customers, staff, suppliers, and authorities are governed by thousands of contracts in contemporary businesses. However, few businesses actually comprehend the dangers or material included in their own contracts.

Dense legalese frequently contains *hidden clauses, unclear terminology, and out-of-date duties,* which pose an unseen threat to profitability and compliance.

AI joined this field as an x-ray of the corporate body, showing things that human eyes would miss, rather than as a substitute for attorneys.

3.2. From Human Evaluation to Automated Diligence

Contract evaluation was one of the most labour-intensive legal activities for many years. During mergers, acquisitions, or audits, teams of colleagues searched through records, frequently under extreme time pressure. It was really expensive. Deloitte Legal (2018) states that up to 50% of M&A legal fees may go toward due diligence.

This procedure was changed with the introduction of machine learning. AI systems were able to quickly identify terms, classify risks, and highlight abnormalities by training algorithms on large datasets of contracts. *Automated Contract Analysis* (ACA) was born out of this change.

Case Study: Legal Data Mining's Ascent and Kira Systems

> Kira Systems was established in Toronto in 2011 and went on to become a leader in this field. Its software recognized more than a thousand different types of terms, including confidentiality and non-compete clauses, indemnities, and termination clauses, using supervised machine learning. Kira was used by international law firms like DLA Piper and Clifford Chance to speed up due diligence investigations in significant mergers.
>
> Kira cut the review time from weeks to just a few hours in one transaction that involved over 50,000 contracts. Additionally, accuracy increased: the algorithm maintained continuous precision over hundreds of pages in situations where human fatigue might lead to overlooks.

This was augmentation, not just automation. From reading documents to analysing computer insights, the lawyer's function has changed throughout time.

3.3. The COIN Revolution at JPMorgan

One of the first and most significant uses of AI in legal and financial operations is the COIN (*Contract Intelligence*) revolution at JPMorgan Chase. COIN is an AI-powered platform that was introduced in 2017 with the purpose of analysing and interpreting commercial loan agreements, a task that previously needed thousands of hours from lawyers and loan officers.

According to reports, it took more than 360,000 people hours a year to examine such contracts for compliance and risk assessment prior to COIN. That workload was cut to seconds with the implementation of COIN, resulting in significant cost savings, a decrease in errors, and improved operational efficiency.

COIN, which is powered by natural language processing (NLP) and machine learning, can:

- *Identify abnormalities and possible hazards;*
- *Standardize legal data for quicker decision-making; and*
- *Extract important legal terms and obligations from complex contracts.*

The way financial institutions handle legal documentation underwent a paradigm shift as a result of this endeavour. It showed that for ordinary, high-volume contract analysis, AI might not only help lawyers but also outperform them in terms of speed and accuracy. *The success of COIN led to the widespread use of comparable AI contract analysis tools in the international banking and legal industries, ushering in what many refer to as the automation era of legal intelligence.*

The ramifications were significant. Error rates decreased, compliance increased, and human attorneys were reallocated to higher-value assignments. *Algorithms that never sleep now accomplish tasks that once required armies of paralegals.* COIN established the standard for corporate legal transformation by proving that AI could lower operational risk in addition to saving money and time. It reinterpreted the concept of efficiency in legal operations.

Essentially, the COIN project came to represent the intersection of AI and law, where technology transforms legal professionals' roles from manual reviewers to strategic analysts.

3.4. The Blockchain Revolution and Smart Contracts

Blockchain technology completely rethought contracts, while machine learning optimized them. *The smart contract is a self-executing digital contract that is automatically enforced when certain criteria are met. Its terms are encoded directly into code.*

Smart contracts, which were first developed by Nick Szabo in the 1990s and subsequently made popular by the Ethereum blockchain, allow for trustless transactions without the need for middlemen. *The contract automatically transfers money, grants rights, or sets off actions if the specified terms are met.*

Case Study: The DAO and the Self-Ruling Code

> The most well-known blockchain-based governance experiment was the DAO (Decentralized Autonomous Organization) in 2016. Through a smart contract intended to manage venture capital investment in a democratic manner, it raised more than $150 million in Ether. However, a bug in the coding made it possible for a hacker to steal $60 million, causing the Ethereum blockchain to undergo an unprecedented "hard fork."
>
> The event demonstrated the potential and danger of smart contracts: who determines intent when "code is law"?
>
> *The DAO reminded the world that human judgment is still necessary for context, purpose, and justice; legal enforceability cannot be reduced to a few lines of code.*

3.5. Hybrid Contracts: Connecting Clause and Code

Hybrid models that combined traditional legal language with digital automation arose as smart contracts gained popularity. Named after Ian Grigg's framework, these "Ricardian Contracts" encode both machine-executable instructions and human-readable phrases.

For instance, a supply chain contract may have both blockchain-based triggers for payment upon confirmed delivery and a conventional indemnity provision. The objective is to create living contracts that are self-monitoring and self-enforcing, not to do away with attorneys.

While governments like Singapore's Infocomm Media Development Authority (IMDA) are experimenting with blockchain for cross-border document authentication, corporations like IBM and Maersk have tested blockchain-based trade finance platforms.

3.6. The Global Compliance Wave

By monitoring changing regulatory requirements, AI-driven contract systems from the Global Compliance Wave also promote global compliance. Thousands of businesses had to update contracts when data privacy laws like California's CCPA and the EU's GDPR were passed. Automated solutions were offered by platforms such as Luminance, ThoughtRiver, and Evisort, which identified impacted clauses and recommended changes.

Slaughter & May, for example, used Luminance to audit GDPR readiness across its clientele, cutting the time from months to days. Generative AI, which can identify hazards and suggest revised language that complies with existing regulations, is increasingly powering these technologies.

Compliance in the future will be proactive rather than reactive, foreseeing changes before they happen.

3.7. The Morality of Automated Contracts

At the nexus of law, technology, and human judgment, the morality of automated contracts—often referred to as *Smart Contracts*—raises significant ethical issues. Without the need for middlemen or human monitoring, these blockchain and AI-powered contracts automatically execute terms whenever predetermined conditions are satisfied.

Although they provide speed, transparency, and trustless execution, moral questions about intent, responsibility, and justice emerge:

- **Insufficient Human Judgment**: Conventional contracts permit judges or negotiators to interpret them morally and fairly. However, automated contracts are inflexible and lack discretion or empathy, even when conditions alter.
- **Accountability and Blame:** It can be difficult to determine who is legally or morally accountable when a smart contract malfunctions or causes harm—the programmer, the deployer, or the AI system.
- **Ethical Programming**: Any bias or unethical rule incorporated into the code becomes law-like and self-enforcing because smart contracts only follow written logic. This raises questions around algorithmic morality.
- **Consent and Understanding:** The ethical precept of informed consent may be called into question by the fact that many users may not fully understand the technical or legal ramifications of automated agreements.

The morality of automated contracts essentially raises the question of whether justice can exist in the absence of human judgment. *AI increases accuracy, but it also runs the risk of depriving contracts of their human moral fabric—the justice, context, and compassion that form the foundation of ethical law.* Creating systems that combine automation and moral responsibility while preventing efficiency from taking precedence over equality is the task that lies ahead.

Thus, automation creates new moral and legal conundrums:

- *Can a party still allege coercion, error, or deception if a smart contract runs automatically?*
- *What happens if the algorithm performs exactly as coded but not as intended, or worse, if it malfunctions?*

The International Chamber of Commerce (ICC) and the UN Commission on International Trade Law (UNCITRAL) are presently investigating frameworks to balance digital enforceability with conventional concepts of consent, intent, and recourse. Meanwhile, courts are starting to deal with these conflicts. The 2019 Singapore International Commercial Court ruling in BCY v. BCZ acknowledged that traditional offer and acceptance rules must still be met when contracts are formed in digital contexts.

Algorithmic accountability becomes just as important as contractual certainty in this new environment.

3.8. Legal Practices in the Automation Age

Artificial Intelligence (AI), machine learning, and process automation are driving a significant revolution of the legal profession in the Automation Age. *Intelligent systems that can quickly and accurately do complicated legal tasks are gradually supplementing or replacing traditional legal processes,* which were formerly characterized by manual investigation, document review, and courtroom representation.

Important changes include:

- **Automated Legal Research**: Artificial intelligence (AI) systems like as Casetext's CoCounsel and LexisNexis's Ravel Law now do real-time legal research, evaluating case law and precedents more quickly and correctly than human paralegals.
- **Contract Automation**: By automating contract drafting, analysis, and risk detection, platforms like Kira Systems and JPMorgan's COIN significantly reduce turnaround times and human error.
- **Predictive Analytics**: In order to guide legal strategy with data-driven insight, courts and law firms are utilizing AI to forecast case outcomes, judge patterns, and settlement probability.
- **Virtual Law Firms:** Chatbots and digital assistants manage client intake, compliance, and even preliminary consultations in remote, AI-assisted legal services made possible by automation.

But new ethical and professional issues are brought forth by this technological advancement. Instead of focusing on mundane paperwork, lawyers must adjust to jobs that emphasize strategic interpretation, monitoring, and ethical stewardship. *In order to ensure that automated systems maintain justice, privacy, and fairness, the profession is moving from "doing law" to "designing legal intelligence."*

AI is altering the delivery of legal services rather than taking the place of attorneys. AI-driven transaction centres are now run by the biggest companies in the world, including PwC Legal, Clifford Chance, and Allen & Overy. These hubs, which frequently incorporate technologies like Harvey AI or Casetext CoCounsel, use machine intelligence to evaluate, categorize, and create contracts at scale.

As AI allows for remote, automated review across jurisdictions, the growth of Legal Process Outsourcing (LPO) has likewise accelerated. Contract analysis is now quicker, less expensive, and more uniform thanks to this global workflow, but it also presents new concerns regarding client confidentiality, data sovereignty, and jurisdictional control.

Essentially, *the goal of legal practice in the automation era is to redefine the role of lawyers in a world where algorithms and lawyers are now working together to achieve justice, rather than to replace them.*

3.9. The Future: Quantum Verification and Autonomous Contracting

In the future, autonomous contracting ecosystems—networks of machine agents that negotiate, carry out, and enforce agreements without human oversight—may result from the convergence of AI, blockchain, and quantum computing. For instance, quantum-secure contracts might be used in smart cities to control traffic systems or energy grids in real time.

But as automation increases, the basic question remains: who is responsible when robots make decisions that are legally binding? The law must change from regulating instruments to regulating systems, where businesses, code, and people all have varying degrees of agency.

Conclusion: Code as Law, Contracts as Code

Contract analysis has changed over time, moving from manual labour to intelligent automation and from paper to pixels. Blockchain and AI have strengthened the law rather than weakened it by integrating legal thinking into every aspect of digital life. However, trust is still the fundamental component of the contract in this new paradigm. The force of the contract, whether it is written in ink or encoded in silicon, rests in the shared belief that justice will be served and promises will be honoured.

As algorithms start to help judges shape rulings, forecast outcomes, and redefine legal fairness, the next chapter examines how this faith is being extended to the courtroom itself.

The era of smart agreements has arrived.

Predictive judgments are the next frontier. When algorithms acquire the ability to make decisions.

Chapter 4: Predictive Decisions: When Algorithms Acquire the Ability to Make Decisions

4.1. The Rise of Algorithmic Adjudication

The point at which facts, evidence, and moral interpretation come together to make a decision is called **judgment**, and it represents the pinnacle of legal reasoning. *This process has been exclusively human for centuries, driven by conscience, empathy, and precedent.* However, as artificial intelligence advances, robots are starting to engage in and sometimes even predict the process of judicial reasoning itself.

With the help of statistical modelling and machine learning, predictive justice systems can now predict case outcomes with amazing accuracy. They trace court behaviour, examine thousands of previous rulings, and even deduce how certain arguments can affect a decision. Data points are being used to chart the probabilities of the once-mystical art of judgment.

This progression ushers in the era of algorithmic adjudication by informing, enhancing, and occasionally challenging judges rather than trying to replace them.

4.2. From Legal Analytics to Judicial Forecasting

The emergence of *legal analytics* in the early 2000s laid the groundwork for predictive justice. In order to find patterns in judicial behaviour, platforms such as Lex Machina, which was established at Stanford's CodeX Centre, started mining court records.

Lawyers could make data-driven, precise adjustments to their litigation tactics by examining the decisions made by certain judges in patent battles or securities cases.

Judicial forecasting—algorithms that could anticipate, with quantifiable confidence, how courts could determine a case—developed from this analytical method.

Natural language processing was employed in a 2016 study by University College London and the University of Sheffield to forecast the results of cases before the European Court of Human Rights (ECHR). Using only textual analysis of case data and previous rulings, the machine attained 79% accuracy.

The notion that "justice is predictable" changed from theory to quantifiable reality for the first time.

Case Study: COMPAS and the American Debate

> The most well-known and contentious example of predictive adjudication in the United States is still the COMPAS system, which was created by Northpointe (now Equivant) and is used in sentencing and parole decisions in a number of states. In the 2016 case of State v. Loomis (Wisconsin), defendant Eric Loomis claimed that COMPAS violated his constitutional rights because the algorithm suggested a harsh sentence, but the defense was unable to review its internal logic.

In the end, the Wisconsin Supreme Court maintained the application of COMPAS as long as justices recognized its limitations. However, the case raised concerns around the world.

According to ProPublica's investigations, COMPAS demonstrated racial bias by overestimating the likelihood of recidivism for Black defendants and underestimating it for white defendants.

The Loomis case is still significant not because of the outcome but rather because of the moral issues it brought up:

- *Is it possible to cross-examine an algorithm?*
- *Who is accountable for algorithmic errors: the court or the coder?*
- *When human prejudice is reflected in data, is justice still blind?*

4.3. Forecasting Justice in the EU

Strong *principles of human oversight, accountability, and transparency* serve as a framework for the European Union's (EU) integration of Artificial Intelligence (AI) into the legal system. These principles are intended to ensure that technology complements justice rather than replaces it:

1. **Human Supervision**

The EU's strategy highlights that AI should support judges and legal professionals rather than take their place. Decisions pertaining to fundamental rights are kept under human control thanks to human scrutiny. AI tools used in legal contexts must continue to be subject to human assessment, with judges retaining the final say in decision-making, according to the European Commission's Ethics Guidelines for Trustworthy AI (2019). This idea stops "black box justice," in which AI renders decisions that are unclear or unassailable.

1. **Responsibility**

EU policy include accountability procedures to make it possible to identify who is responsible when AI systems make mistakes or cause harm. AI systems employed in justice and law enforcement are categorized as high-risk under the EU AI Act (2024), necessitating stringent adherence to ethical, legal, and data protection criteria. Risk assessments, documentation, and audit trails must be kept up to date by developers and organizations using these AI tools in order to prove compliance and provide remedies in the event that something goes wrong.

1. Transparency and Openness

To keep the public's confidence in AI-driven justice, transparency is essential. Citizens have the right to know how an algorithm affects a court decision, and the EU requires judicial AI systems to be explicable. Automated systems are required by the AI Act and the General Data Protection Regulation (GDPR) to disclose their data sources and logic. This guarantees that AI functions transparently and that its logic may be scrutinized, challenged, or rectified.

As a result, the EU sees AI as a helpful instrument for the judiciary, enhancing consistency, efficiency, and access to justice, but never at the price of justice or human dignity. The EU is creating a framework that keeps algorithmic justice fundamentally human through human oversight, robust accountability systems, and enforced openness.

The European Union has adopted a more cautious but forward-thinking strategy across the Atlantic. The European Commission for the Efficiency of Justice (CEPEJ) began researching "AI in judicial systems" in 2017 with a focus on human oversight, accountability, and openness.

The Predictive Justice Project (France), one of the top academic projects, investigates how machine learning might help judges in administrative and civil disputes. French start-up **Predictice** *estimates case outcomes, such as the likelihood of success and possible damages, using algorithms that have been trained on thousands of court decisions.* Major French law firms and insurers already use it to evaluate lawsuit risk.

Since then, though, the French Constitutional Court has passed stringent rules prohibiting the publication of predictive models of the behaviour of specific judges, claiming that such information could jeopardize judicial independence.

Europe's answer reveals a profound conflict between the sanctity of unbiased judgment and the need for data-driven efficiency.

The EU AI Act, which categorizes AI systems according to risk, and the European Ethical Charter on the use of AI in judicial systems are the main ways that the EU controls the application of AI in the legal system. The objective is to maintain fundamental rights, judicial independence, and justice while promoting innovation.

Important Regulatory Structures

- **The EU AI Act (Regulation (EU) 2024/1689)**: This all-encompassing, risk-based legislation is directly applicable throughout the European Union.
    - **Prohibited AI Practices**: The Act prohibits AI technologies that are deemed to pose a direct threat to fundamental rights, including most real-time remote biometric identification in public areas and government-run social score.
    - Human supervision is required to guarantee that people may step in and make adjustments.
    - **High-Risk AI Systems:** AI systems employed in law enforcement and the administration of justice are typically categorized as high-risk. These systems include those that help with legal interpretation or apply the law to particular facts. Strict requirements apply to these systems, such as:
    - Sufficient risk assessment and mitigation systems.
    - To reduce bias, use representative, high-quality data.
    - **Timeline for Implementation:** Most regulations pertaining to high-risk systems in the judicial sector will become fully operative on August 2, 2026, while

the limitations on unacceptable-risk AI will take effect on February 2, 2025.
    - Thorough activity recording and documentation.
    - Excellent cybersecurity, robustness, and accuracy.
    - **Transparency Requirements:** Artificial intelligence (AI) systems that produce deepfakes or engage with users (such as chatbots) must reveal that the material is AI-generated rather than human.
- **The European Ethics Charter:** This charter, which was approved by the European Commission for the Efficiency of Justice (CEPEJ) of the Council of Europe in 2018, outlined five fundamental guidelines for the application of AI in legal systems:
    - **Principle of Quality and Security:** The models must be created in a secure setting, and the data must originate from approved sources.
    - The "under user control" principle states that human oversight is crucial, that users have the right to object to an AI-driven process, and that users must be informed when interacting with AI.
    - **Principle of Respect for Basic Rights:** The right to a fair trial and other fundamental rights must coexist with AI tools.
    - **Non-Discrimination Principle:** AI must stop discrimination from starting or getting worse.
    - Transparency, impartiality, and fairness principle: External audits should be permitted, and data processing techniques should be easily accessible and comprehensible.

Difficulties and Ethical Issues

There are also serious issues with the use of AI in the legal system:

- **Judicial Independence and Human Oversight**: Judges' independence and impartiality may be jeopardized by an over-reliance on AI "predictive justice" techniques. In order to avoid negative consequences, the EU requires significant human engagement in high-risk applications.
- **Bias and Biases:** If AI algorithms are trained on biased data, there is a chance that they can reinforce or magnify pre-existing biases, creating concerns about impartiality and justice.
- **Confidentiality and Data Protection**: There is a chance that using general-purpose AI systems for legal research would unintentionally reveal private or sensitive case data, which could subsequently be utilized to train the AI models.

  By creating a clear legal and moral framework that puts human rights and trust first, the EU's strategy seeks to reduce these vulnerabilities.

Current Uses and Advantages

Instead of rendering final judicial decisions, AI is mostly utilized to increase productivity and help legal practitioners with administrative and research chores.

- **Administrative Efficiency:** Tasks like resource allocation, case management, and document anonymisation/ pseudonymisation are automated using tools.
- **Access to Justice:** AI-powered virtual assistants and translation tools can lower language barriers and make it easier for the general public and legal experts to navigate information.
- **Legal Research and Document Analysis**: AI can quickly examine enormous volumes of statutes, case law, and legal documents, finding pertinent material and producing summaries to help judges and attorneys.

4.4. The Smart Court Ecosystem in China

China is the nation that has developed predictive justice in the most methodical way. The Supreme People's Court oversaw the development of the Smart Court System, which incorporates AI at all judicial levels. The system generates preliminary views, classifies cases automatically, suggests legal provisions, and even forecasts probable verdicts.

Case Study: The Hangzhou Internet Court

The Hangzhou Internet Court was founded in 2017 and deals with cases involving digital copyrights, online contracts, and e-commerce. Its artificial intelligence technology, dubbed the "Judicial Brain," examines case files, recommends pertinent statutes, and verifies rulings against national precedents. Although they still have the last say, judges mainly rely on AI for direction.

Over 100 million cases have been processed digitally by Chinese smart courts by 2024, with an average 30% reduction in case times. However, given the centralization of judicial data, foreign observers voice concerns about political interference and transparency. Predictive adjudication at scale has both potential and risk, as China's program illustrates.

4.5. The Promise: Reliability, Effectiveness, and Availability

AI has enormous potential to improve the judicial system's availability, efficacy, and dependability—three essential components of a contemporary and easily accessible legal system.

Dependability

In routine or data-intensive jobs like legal research, case law retrieval, and document review, AI systems can process enormous volumes of legal data with surprising consistency, reducing human mistake and prejudice. AI can provide predictable and repeatable results when built with transparent algorithms and high-quality, representative datasets, enhancing the overall dependability of legal reasoning support. Strict compliance requirements under the AI Act, which requires ongoing testing, monitoring, and validation to verify that AI tools function as intended without unanticipated deviations, are used in the EU to assure reliability.

Efficiency

By cutting down on delays, optimizing operations, and promoting well-informed decision-making, AI improves judicial efficacy. Predictive analytics and automated document drafting tools are examples of systems that can relieve judges and clerks of tedious administrative tasks so they may concentrate on intricate legal interpretation and decision-making. Furthermore, the quality and coherence of court rulings are strengthened by AI's capacity to identify contradictions, cross-reference precedents, and offer pertinent legal arguments. This effectiveness helps make the legal system quicker, more economical, and more data-driven.

Availability

Platforms powered by AI have the potential to increase justice's accessibility and inclusivity. Natural language interfaces, virtual legal assistants, and online dispute resolution systems enable citizens to access legal services and information around-the-clock, removing barriers related to cost, location, and language. Through its Digital Europe Programme and e-Justice initiatives, the EU encourages this kind of digital change with the goal of ensuring that all citizens, regardless of location or socioeconomic level, may interact with the legal system in a convenient and equitable manner.

Building a dependable, efficient, and widely accessible justice ecosystem—*one in which technology enhances human judgment, expedites access to legal remedies, and supports the rule of law in a digital age*—is essentially the promise of artificial intelligence in the judiciary.

Predictive justice proponents contend that AI can improve the consistency, effectiveness, and accessibility of court rulings:

- **Consistency**: AI reduces the randomness that frequently underlies sentence discrepancies by spotting patterns in precedent.
- **Efficiency**: By speeding up case management, predictive tools allow judges to concentrate on sophisticated reasoning rather than minute procedural issues.
- **Access to Justice:** By using predictive models to forecast

results before to bringing cases, citizens and attorneys can cut down on needless litigation and expenses.

Predictive AI has the potential to transform judicial efficiency in developing nations where case backlogs often last for years.

To cut down on delays and corruption, pilot programs under Kenya's Judiciary Transformation Framework and India's eCourts system are already investigating data-driven docket administration.

4.6. The Dangers: Dehumanization, Transparency, and Bias

However, *every benefit has a shadow*. The data used to train predictive algorithms is reflected in them, and historical legal data is not impartial. Algorithms run the potential of encoding and magnifying biases present in prior rulings, racial inequities in punishment, and gender imbalances in adjudication.

Furthermore, the majority of AI models function as "black boxes," meaning that even their developers are unable to understand their decision-making processes. Opacity is unacceptable in the legal field, which is based on logic and justification. Fairness and comprehensibility are both necessary for justice. The validity of justice is undermined if someone cannot understand why they were found guilty or denied parole.

The danger of dehumanization comes last. *Courts are moral theatres where narratives, feelings, and context are important; they are not just logical machines.* Over-reliance on prediction analytics runs the risk of marginalizing human empathy in favour of probabilistic certainty.

4.7. The Search for Explainable Justice (XAI)

The requirement for accountability and openness in the legal decision-making process of AI systems is central to the Search for *Explainable Justice*. The idea of Explainable Artificial Intelligence (XAI) has become crucial to maintaining the fundamentals of justice as algorithms help with sentencing, bail decisions, and predictive policing.

AI models, particularly deep learning systems, frequently function as "black boxes," generating results without obvious logic. This lack of explainability puts basic legal concepts like due process, justice, and the right to appeal at jeopardy. Trust in the legal system declines if judges and defendants are unable to comprehend the reasoning behind an algorithm's decision.

Therefore, the goal of Explainable Justice is to make sure that:

- *Humans can comprehend and contest AI conclusions;*
- *Judicial transparency is preserved, enabling legal actors to follow the reasoning behind AI outputs;*
- *Discrimination and bias ingrained in algorithms can be found and fixed;*
- *Humans, not computers, continue to bear ethical responsibility.*

XAI is a means of bringing machine reasoning into line with legal reasoning by serving as a link between algorithmic accuracy and human comprehension. *Explainable justice guarantees that technology supports, not replaces, the rule of law in the new era of AI-augmented law.*

Researchers and legislators support Explainable Artificial Intelligence (XAI) in legal systems as a means of resolving these conflicts. Like a judge writing a reasoned decision, an explainable model must demonstrate how each variable contributed to an outcome.

Justice is categorized as a "high-risk domain" under the European Union's AI Act (2024), which requires human control, traceability, and openness. In a similar vein, accountability procedures are required by the UNESCO Recommendation on AI Ethics and the OECD Principles on AI to guarantee that AI systems in law continue to be auditable and contestable.

Instead of giving up on predictive tools, the objective is to incorporate them into a constitutional framework for algorithmic responsibility so that robots support justice rather than replace it.

Case Study: The AI Judge Initiative in Estonia

> An AI-driven adjudication system for minor claims under €7,000 has been tested by Estonia, a global leader in digital government. Based on information provided via a secure web gateway, the AI makes first decisions. The ability to appeal before a human judge is still available to litigants.
>
> The Estonian project, albeit still in its pilot phase, embodies a daring idea: justice as a service that is easily accessible, effective, and technologically advanced. It poses important queries on how appeals, accountability, and legal reasoning will change in a hybrid system, as well as the future division of labour between human and machine judges.

4.8. The Human Factor: Judgement beyond Calculation

In the end, judgment is more important than facts. *Although machines are capable of computing probabilities, they are unable to assess moral value or understand regret.* Justice involves more than just forecasting results; it also involves interpreting meaning. A human is the only one who can determine what ought to occur; an algorithm may predict what is likely to occur.

Therefore, symbiosis—*a collaboration in which humans uphold principles and robots reveal patterns*—is the most promising concept of predictive adjudication rather than replacement. The future judge might be seated next to a knowledgeable assistant rather than a competitor; a digital conscience that counsels rather than makes decisions.

4.9. The Path Ahead: From Forecasting to Convincing

Systems that not only forecast decisions but also help formulate arguments—tools that comprehend the art of persuasion itself—represent the next frontier. In real time, generative AI systems are already learning to create briefs, mimic opposing viewpoints, and provide counter-precedents.

The distinction between advocacy and analytics will become hazier as time goes on, posing new moral and constitutional dilemmas. Will litigation turn into an algorithmic battle if both parties use AI to predict and plan?

This is the paradox of predictive justice: *the human element of the law must become more intentional as it becomes more data-driven.*

Conclusion: The Soul of Law and the Algorithmic Judge

Predictive adjudication is situated at the intersection of science and philosophy, efficiency and ethics. It threatens to automate one of humanity's most fundamental moral functions, but it also promises to make justice quicker, more equitable, and more consistent.

Designing systems where data benefits mankind without decreasing human dignity is a challenge for technologists, legislators, and jurists. The last voice must remain human, not because robots are incapable but rather because justice is and must continue to be a moral act, even though algorithmic judges may eventually help in every courtroom.

Chapter 5: AI in Courtrooms – The Future Advocacy and the Digital Bench

5.1. Reimagining the Courtroom

One of the oldest institutions of society is the traditional courtroom, with its solemn benches, robed judges, and hushed onlookers. It is the place where speech, logic, and ritual are manifestations of justice.

However, there is a significant change taking place at this old stage. Automation, digital platforms, and artificial intelligence are changing not just how justice is administered but also how it is perceived.

The contemporary courtroom is developing into a data-driven ecosystem, complete with robotic clerks, AI-assisted judges, virtual hearings, and automated transcribing.

The future advocate might appear before a digital bench, an intelligent infrastructure that records, listens, interprets, and even makes recommendations, rather than just a human judge.

This chapter examines how AI has become an active player in the legal system rather than just a tool.

5.2. The Digital Bench's Ascent

The emergence of the Digital Bench represents a turning point in the development of legal systems, when intelligence, data, and technology come together to support judges' conventional roles. To improve judicial efficiency, consistency, and accessibility, courts throughout the European Union and beyond are gradually adopting digital infrastructure, AI-assisted tools, and data-driven insights.

- **Paper to Platform**

  E-filing portals, virtual hearings, and integrated case management systems have taken the place of laborious paper-based procedures in courtrooms. Real-time case tracking, secure data exchange, and quicker document processing are all made possible by this digital move. Thanks to AI algorithms that synthesize information, identify contradictions, and retrieve pertinent precedents from extensive legal databases, judges may now quickly review whole case histories.

- **Artificial Intelligence as a Court Assistant**

  The goal of the "digital bench" is to empower judges rather than to replace them. Judges can receive insights on case trends, likely outcomes, and comparative legal interpretations via AI-powered judicial assistants, such as automated legal reasoning engines and predictive analytics systems. For example, EU pilot initiatives like France's predictive justice tools and Estonia's digital courts show how AI may improve judicial consistency while preserving human oversight and moral purity.

- **Fairness and Efficiency Combined**

The rise of digital courts also means that cases are processed more quickly and openly, which lowers backlogs and boosts public trust. Because digital records and algorithmic recommendations are auditable, decision-making is kept responsible and traceable. Additionally, internet hearings and AI-assisted translation technologies increase the accessibility of justice for those who live in different places and speak different languages.

- **A New Judicial Culture**

However, a new judicial ethos based on digital literacy, ethical consciousness, and ongoing human control is required in light of this technological advancement. In the digital age, judges need to comprehend not only the law but also the reasoning and constraints of the systems that support them. The European Union's focus on reliable and human-centered AI guarantees that democratic values and fundamental rights continue to serve as the foundation for this transition.

The rise of the Digital Bench signifies the redefining of judicial authority in the digital era, where machine intelligence amplifies human understanding to offer justice that is quicker, more equitable, and firmly rooted in transparency. It is not just a technological advancement.

Virtual case management platforms and electronic file systems marked the beginning of the first wave of courtroom digitization. But as these systems began to think—automating legal reasoning, evaluating evidence, and streamlining trial procedures—true AI integration emerged.

These days, nations like China, Singapore, and the UK run completely digital courts with algorithmic scheduling, evidence submission, and hearings. Judges have access to dashboards that show case summaries, estimated timetables, and even sentiment analysis of earlier rulings.

Launched under its Courts of the Future project, the Singapore Supreme Court's "Smart Courtroom" effort incorporates AI capabilities to help judges summarize evidence and produce preliminary drafts of opinions. *The courtroom itself has become somewhat autonomous, and what started out as administrative efficiency has evolved into a cognitive partnership.*

5.3. AI-Moderated Trials and Virtual Hearings

The COVID-19 epidemic hastened the adoption of virtual hearings around the world, making digital adjudication a permanent feature. However, AI is changing these virtual procedures in ways other than video conferencing, such as:

- Natural language processing (NLP)-driven real-time translation and transcription.
- Speech analytics to identify emotional stress, hesitancy, and tone.
- Automated scheduling that ranks cases according to their complexity and urgency.

Within minutes after a hearing, official court records are now produced in the UK by AI-driven transcription systems, freeing up clerks to work on more valuable projects.

In a similar vein, the Supreme Court eCommittee of India established virtual benches with AI translators to overcome linguistic barriers across the country's 23 official languages.

Systems like Verbit and FTR RealTime are used by a number of US jurisdictions to generate searchable digital transcripts that interface with case management systems. In addition to increasing productivity, the technology increases accessibility and transparency, especially for those with disabilities.

Case Study: South Korea's AI Judge's Assistant

An AI system that evaluates court documents, condenses information, and suggests pertinent precedents for judges was introduced by the Supreme Court of Korea in 2022. The "U-Justice" engine processes thousands of rulings using deep learning to generate succinct briefs that significantly cut down on case preparation time.

Judges claim that by bringing up points they may have missed, U-Justice improves the calibre of deliberation. However, worries regarding over-reliance continue to exist: *might algorithmic recommendations inadvertently skew judicial reasoning?*

A common paradox in AI-assisted law is demonstrated by South Korea's model: the more effective the technology, the more subtly it affects human judgment.

5.4. Automation in Legal Representation: The AI Advocate

Beyond the bench, AI is changing advocacy as an art form. These days, intelligent assistants draft briefs, evaluate competing viewpoints, and recommend case tactics.

- **The Phenomenon of DoNotPay**

Joshua Browder's *DoNotPay*, branded "the world's first robot lawyer," tried to use artificial intelligence (AI) to argue a traffic case in a U.S. courtroom in 2023 using an earphone before being prohibited for practicing law without authorization. Even though the event was problematic from a legal standpoint, it represented a future in which AI might work alongside attorneys as co-counsel rather than as a substitute.

- **Litigation Analytics and Law Firms**

AI systems like Harvey, Luminance, and Kira Systems are currently used by large companies like Baker McKenzie, Allen & Overy, and Clifford Chance for due diligence, legal drafting, and evidence review. Massive amounts of discovery materials, including emails, contracts, and financial records, are analysed by these computers to find trends, irregularities, or contradictions that human attorneys might overlook.

Predictive analytics systems evaluate previous decisions made by the same judge or court in order to estimate the likelihood of success in litigation. Strategies that were previously based on experience and intuition are now measured.

- **Analytics of Evidence: When AI Becomes a Witness**

Once a niche field, digital forensics is now essential to court procedures. AI now reconstructs events by analysing digital trails, voice records, and video footage. Voice analysis assesses sincerity or deceit trends; deepfake detection techniques authenticate digital evidence; and facial recognition recognizes suspects in surveillance footage.

U.S. prosecutors employed AI-enhanced picture verification in Commonwealth v. John Doe (a pseudonym used for privacy) in 2020 to verify the authenticity of altered CCTV footage. The defense questioned how an algorithm's "confidence score" could be cross-examined, raising concerns about the system's interpretability.

This case highlighted a significant change: the courtroom is now discussing data interpretation systems in addition to facts.

Case Study: China's Courtroom AI Recorder

Natural language processing is used by China's Intelligent Trial Support System, which is interconnected across multiple provinces, to record and summarize hearings. The AI hears testimony, creates transcripts, and draws attention to contradictions with earlier claims.

Judges are given on-screen suggestions regarding pertinent statutes or previous instances in certain trials. Attorneys have access to AI-generated summaries of cross-examinations, which include likelihood scores for important facts that are supported or refuted.

The so-called "Judicial Brain" has improved productivity but also made it harder to distinguish between observation and decision-making. Opponents caution that these instruments could softly influence decisions by subtly changing judge perception.

5.5. Constitutional and Ethical Consequences

The introduction of AI into the legal system calls into question a number of fundamental justice principles:

1. **Due Process and Transparency**: *Can plaintiffs want to review the algorithm's logic if an AI drafts or influences a judgment?*
2. **Right to a Fair Hearing**: *If one party employs sophisticated analytics and the other does not, how can equality of weapons be upheld?*
3. **Admissibility of AI Evidence**: *Under evidentiary norms, can an AI's conclusion be regarded as expert testimony?*
4. **Judicial Independence**: *Where does human judgment end and computer thinking begin if judges heavily rely on algorithmic support? Does machine thinking start when human judgment ends?*

These worries are real. As was previously said, the U.S. Supreme Court was compelled to consider whether opaque AI suggestions violated constitutional rights in State v. Loomis (2016). The EU AI Act, which labels "AI systems in judicial contexts" as high-risk and requires stringent human monitoring, has sparked similar discussions throughout Europe.

5.6. Africa's Digital Courtroom: A Leapfrog Prospect

AI-driven digital courtrooms are poised to revolutionize Africa's justice systems, which have long been hampered by scarce resources and sluggish case backlogs. African countries have the chance to go straight into next-generation legal technologies, eschewing antiquated infrastructure in favour of cloud-based justice platforms, e-filing, remote hearings, and AI-assisted rulings, in contrast to developed countries saddled by legacy systems.

Judges can concentrate on important matters by using AI tools to automate repetitive legal activities like case scheduling, transcription, and evidence classification. In order to promote efficiency and fairness, predictive analytics could help evaluate case trends and sentencing consistency.

A shift toward smart justice is already evident on the continent as nations like **South Africa, Kenya,** and **Rwanda** are testing digital case management systems and virtual courts. But there are still issues, especially with regard to algorithmic bias, infrastructure limitations, data privacy, and digital literacy.

Africa's digital courtroom revolution has the potential to improve access to justice, decrease corruption, and establish a transparent, tech-enabled judicial environment if it is applied properly. This may turn a long-standing weakness into a global model of innovation.

AI in courtrooms presents a previously unheard-of chance to overcome conventional inefficiencies in emerging nations.

- **Nigeria:** AI-powered document automation speeds up backlog clearance in Nigeria.
- **Kenya:** AI-powered case management and transcription are used by Kenya's Judiciary's *Digital Justice System* for virtual hearings, especially in land and business disputes.

- **Zambia**: Additionally, the Ministry of Justice in Zambia is conducting pilot programs to investigate automated registry maintenance and electronic case referencing, which are first steps toward a digital bench.

These initiatives showcase a distinct advantage for Africa: rising judiciaries may create AI-native judicial frameworks from the ground up instead of updating existing systems.

5.7. The Digital Bench's Psychology

The psychological component of AI integration is one that is often disregarded. When they are aware that machines are watching, recording, or offering advice, judges, attorneys, and litigants react differently. *According to research from the University of Cambridge (2021), judges who receive AI assistance are more consistent but have less faith in their own judgment.*

In a similar vein, litigants frequently believe that AI-enhanced courts are less sympathetic but more impartial. Data is redefining the ritual of justice, which has historically been based on human gravitas.

Thus, the digital bench poses an important question: *Can justice maintain its human legitimacy in a setting mediated by machines?*

Case Study: Brazil's Virtual Supreme Court

> In order to categorize and rank incoming appeals, Brazil's Supreme Federal Court (STF) introduced an AI system dubbed Victor in 2024. To lessen the backlog in the courts, Victor examines petitions, finds precedents, and suggests case grouping.
>
> Victor reduced delays by over half by processing more than 300,000 appeals by 2025. However, the court carefully restricts Victor's involvement to clerical support—a purposeful barrier that upholds human judgment. A practical paradigm is provided by Brazil's experience: AI as an intelligent filter rather than a decision-maker.

5.8. From Robot Judges to Cognitive Justice

AI will increasingly influence judicial reasoning, not by replacing it but by augmenting it. The next stage will see cognitive justice systems, where machine learning, natural language reasoning, and emotional analytics come together to mimic human deliberation. Imagine a "virtual assistant" that can summarize each party's argument in both legal and moral terms, identify precedent relevance, and flag potential ethical conflicts. Prototypes of these systems are already being developed at the Chinese Academy of Sciences and the Stanford CodeX Centre.

Conclusion: The Machine Bench and the Future Advocate

The courtroom of the future will be a networked intelligence, where computational accuracy and human reasoning coexist, rather than just a geographical location. Justice will take place in hybrid environments that cut across time and space, judges will deliberate with algorithmic intelligence, and attorneys will prepare arguments based on data analytics.

But despite all of these changes, one thing never changes: justice is still a human endeavour. The machine can help with thought, but it is not capable of feeling conscience. Consistency is predictable, but compassion is not.

Therefore, the challenge is not whether AI will enter our courts—it has already done so—but rather how to maintain the moral spirit of justice in a digital mind. We examine this deeper philosophical frontier in the upcoming chapter, Algorithmic Ethics and the Moral Limits of Machine Judgment, where technology, philosophy, and law converge to define justice in the era of artificial intelligence.

Chapter 6: Algorithmic Ethics and the Moral Limits of Machine Judgment

Introduction: Law, Morality, and Machines

One of the most significant changes in human civilization occurs at the nexus of morality, law, and machinery. Law has been a uniquely human endeavour for ages; it is based on reason, directed by moral judgment, and upheld by social consensus. However, the development of artificial intelligence (AI) is upending this antiquated system and casting doubt on our comprehension of what it means to interpret, make decisions, and administer justice.

Algorithms are being used more and more in today's legal systems to evaluate contracts, forecast case results, and even help with sentencing. Previously just used as documentation tools, machines are now actively involved in legal reasoning. Important problems are brought up by this evolution:

- *Can an algorithm comprehend fairness?*
- *Should morality be interpreted by a machine? And,*
- *When digital bias takes the place of human bias or even reinforces it, how can we guarantee justice?*

A careful balance between efficiency and ethics is at the centre of this change. The law must maintain its moral compass—its ability to consider human intent, compassion, and context—even as AI promises quicker, more consistent conclusions. In order to ensure that legal automation benefits people rather than replacing them, the issue is not just to digitize justice but also to humanize technology.

As we move into this new era, the convergence of morality, law, and technology forces us to rethink justice as a living system that can change with the sophisticated tools it now uses, rather than as a static institution.

Justice has always been a moral endeavour, based not only on rules but also on values: *fairness, proportionality, empathy, and social responsibility*. When algorithms enter the courtroom, they bring efficiency and consistency—but also new ethical challenges. This chapter explores the moral limits of AI in law, looking at how ethical theories can guide the design, deployment, and oversight of algorithmic legal systems.

6.1. Moral Structures for Algorithmic Judgement

The issue of moral framework becomes inevitable as artificial intelligence starts to play a role in legal decision-making. Algorithms are capable of processing enormous amounts of legal data and making decisions quickly and consistently, but if they lack a moral compass, they run the risk of becoming into impersonal, cold, logical tools. After all, law is about ideals as much as laws.

Societies must establish ethical frameworks that direct AI systems' interpretation and application of legal rules in order to include morality into algorithmic judgment. These frameworks are derived from established philosophical traditions:

- *Deontological ethics guarantees that algorithms respect human rights and procedural justice by emphasizing duty and loyalty to the law.*
- *Consequentialist ethics, which emphasizes results, can assist AI systems in optimizing for social welfare, damage reduction, or fairness.*
- *Algorithms must represent the honesty and compassion of the cultures they serve, according to virtue ethics, which is based on moral character.*

Value alignment—training systems on data and concepts that represent democratic norms, equality before the law, and the preservation of human dignity—is another aspect of developing moral frameworks for AI judgment. This calls for ethical supervision, open code, and multidisciplinary cooperation between legal experts, philosophers, and technologists.

In the end, algorithmic judgment must function within the bounds of human morality rather than taking its place. Humanity may develop systems that are both intelligent and just by incorporating ethical reasoning into legal AI, where technology enhances rather than distorts our quest for justice.

6.1.1. **Utilitarianism: Optimizing the Common Good**

The greatest good for the largest number is how utilitarian ethics assesses choices. Because AI systems can foresee societal consequences and model probability, they are well suited to utilitarian reasoning.

Case Study: Using Predictive Policing

Predictive policing technologies, such as the Crime Anticipation System and PredPol, were created in the Netherlands and the United Kingdom to effectively distribute police resources, potentially lowering overall crime. Targeting high-risk areas improves public safety from a utilitarian standpoint.

However, there are ethical problems with this strategy. Data-driven targeting has a disproportionately negative effect on underrepresented communities by reinforcing previous biases. Even if total crime may decline, some groups may be disproportionately affected, exposing a conflict between justice as fairness and utilitarian efficiency.

6.1.2. **Deontology: Obligation and Regulations over Repercussions**

Deontological ethics places more emphasis on following laws, obligations, and values than on results. This approach, when applied to AI, requires that systems uphold moral obligations, legal requirements, and human rights regardless of anticipated results.

Case Study: COMPAS in U.S. Sentencing

Sentencing judgments are influenced by the COMPAS system's prediction of recidivism risk. From a deontological perspective, it might be against the responsibility to guarantee transparency and due process to determine someone's liberty using a proprietary, opaque algorithm. COMPAS may violate fairness and procedural justice norms even if it lowers overall recidivism (a utilitarian good).

6.1.3. Virtue Ethics: Moral Judgment, Wisdom, And Character

Actions are judged under virtue ethics according to their moral character and practical knowledge (phronesis). The problem with AI is clear: computers don't have consciousness, experience, or empathy.

Case Study: The DAO Smart Contract (2016)

When The DAO's smart contract was compromised, it executed transactions without taking fairness or intent into account, following its code faithfully. A vital lesson is highlighted by virtue ethics: AI systems are unable to absorb justice as a moral virtue. To stop algorithmic activity that is morally defective but legally correct, human monitoring is still necessary.

6.2. Explainability and Transparency

Explainability and Transparency are the pillars of confidence in the era of algorithmic justice. *Society needs to comprehend how and why artificial intelligence systems arrive at their results as they increasingly support legal reasoning, whether through contract assessments, sentence recommendations, or predictive analytics.* Justice runs the risk of turning into a mysterious system that even the people it serves cannot access without explanation.

Explainability *is the capacity of an AI system to explain its reasoning in words that humans can comprehend.* Judges, attorneys, and litigants should be able to follow an algorithm's logic, assess the sources of its evidence, and challenge its presumptions in legal situations. The rule of law, which demands responsibility and rational explanation, is irreconcilable with an AI that is incapable of explaining itself.

Transparency is more profound and *encompasses openness in AI system design, data, and governance.* This entails revealing the training datasets, the factors affecting results, and the precautions taken to avoid bias or manipulation. Oversight and public criticism are made possible by transparent mechanisms, which strengthen due process and legitimacy.

The difficulty is striking a balance between national security, data privacy, and intellectual property. Even when algorithms are used as a mediator, legal AI must nevertheless function under the tenet that justice must not only be served but also be perceived as being served.

Explainability and transparency are ultimately moral requirements rather than technological extras. They safeguard the integrity of the legal system in a world where machines are increasingly in charge by ensuring that algorithmic justice is still subject to human judgment.

Algorithmic transparency is a fundamental ethical principle. AI's decision-making process must be understood by courts, litigants, and society at large. A developing field that tackles this issue is explainable AI (XAI).

Case Study: AI Judge Pilot in Estonia

> Transparency is emphasized in Estonia's small claim e-judge system. Litigants have the option to appeal to a human judge, and AI-generated suggestions are fully auditable. Estonia shows that ethical AI in law necessitates both performance and responsibility by incorporating explainability.

6.3. Data Ethics, Fairness, and Bias

Data ethics are important to algorithmic justice's integrity. Every AI system is only as fair as the data it learns from, and in the legal field, where decisions have a significant moral impact on people's lives, liberties, and reputations, this is especially true. Data ethics ensures that technical efficiency never takes precedence over the values of equality and fairness by regulating how lawful AI systems gather, process, and interpret data.

Bias can enter an algorithm in a number of ways, such as through imbalanced datasets that over-represent particular groups, historical data that reflects human prejudice, or design decisions made by developers who are ignorant of their own presumptions. Such bias can reinforce or even magnify discrimination when it is ingrained in legal AI, resulting in unfair contract evaluations, disproportionate sentencing, or unfair bail judgments.

Fairness needs to be built into the system in order to combat this:

- *Why Representative Datasets that represent social diversity rather than historical exclusion are necessary for ethical AI in law.*

- *Before implementation, algorithmic audits are used to identify and address unfair tendencies.*
- *Ethical monitoring organizations that guarantee ongoing responsibility and adherence to human rights norms.*
- *Human-in-the-loop systems, which enable machine recommendations to be improved by moral and contextual judgment.*

Data ethics is a moral commitment to justice rather than just a technological field. Societies can guarantee that AI strengthens rather than weakens the fundamental promise of law: *equality before justice, by openly addressing bias and placing a high priority on fairness at every level of design and implementation.*

AI programs pick up knowledge from past data. Algorithms run the potential of escalating injustice if prior decisions are biased.

Case Study: COMPAS Analysis by ProPublica (2016)

> According to ProPublica, COMPAS underestimated the likelihood of recidivism for white offenders while overestimating it for Black defendants. This illustrates algorithmic bias in action and emphasizes the ethical need to regularly examine and improve prediction models.
>
> Using fairness restrictions during model training, curating representative and diverse datasets, and maintaining ongoing human oversight and review are all part of mitigating bias.
>
> Fairness is an ethical requirement that cannot be compromised. The legitimacy of the legal system is undermined by a mechanism that regularly misjudges particular groups.

6.4. Independence and Accountability

Independence and accountability are crucial for upholding the rule of law in the developing field of algorithmic justice. As artificial intelligence starts to support—or even impact—legal decisions, society needs to make sure that these systems operate without excessive intervention and continue to be held accountable for their results.

In legal AI, **Independence** refers to *the ability of algorithms to function independently of institutional, commercial, or political interference.* AI systems must be shielded from unconscious prejudices introduced by their creators, financiers, or data sources, just as human judges are supposed to maintain objectivity. To stop the abuse of AI for political or personal advantage, this calls for open auditing procedures, ethical firewalls, and transparent governance structures.

But the ethical opposite of independence is **Accountability**. Even while AI systems are capable of acting independently, their developers, implementers, and supervisors must ultimately take accountability for their decisions. This principle *guarantees that there is always a clear line of culpability in the event that an algorithm makes a mistake or causes harm, ensuring that no choice escapes human review.* Accountability may be enforced across the AI justice pipeline with the use of tools like explainable decision logs, legal traceability, and algorithmic effect evaluations.

Finding the ideal balance between giving AI the autonomy to operate impartially and preserving the human oversight required to respect moral and legal norms is the difficult part.

In this way, independence and accountability—one guaranteeing responsibility, the other guaranteeing fairness—form the two cornerstones of valid algorithmic justice. Together, they protect the moral authority of the law in a time when robots are becoming more and more prevalent.

When an algorithm makes a mistake, who is at fault? In the legal field, where human liberty is at risk, this concern is especially pertinent.

Case Study: The Smart Court System in China

> AI-assisted courts in China compile evidence and draft preliminary rulings. Although judges still have the final say, the courts must consider shared accountability: *if an AI-generated recommendation leads to an incorrect decision, who is responsible—the judge, the developer, or the institution?*
>
> In order to maintain accountability, human actors must ethically maintain the final say in decisions.

6.5. AI and Ethical Boundaries: When Machines Are Unable to Make Judgement

A crucial concern emerges as artificial intelligence becomes more and more integrated into legal procedures: *where should the ethical lines be drawn when robots are entrusted with deciphering morality, justice, and human behaviour*? Even if AI is very good at logic, pattern recognition, and data analysis, it is still fundamentally incapable of moral reasoning, which is the foundation of legal judgment.

Algorithmic Reasoning's Boundaries

AI systems use statistical correlations and mathematical models to operate. They can suggest sentence ranges, forecast probable results, and spot trends in legal data. *They do not, however, comprehend human emotion, context, or intent—factors that frequently influence legal fairness. AI cannot balance equality versus precise legality or compassion against punishment, unlike judges.* It lacks the moral compass necessary to understand justice in the context of society as a whole.

Practical Ethical Boundaries

These boundaries are acknowledged by European legal systems. Systems employed in law enforcement and justice are categorized as high-risk under the EU AI Act, which means that significant human control is always required. *Judges, not automated results, must continue to be the last arbiters of justice. AI may help make judgments, but it must never make decisions on its own.* This is a clear ethical barrier. This guarantees that moral responsibility, which cannot be codified, stays firmly in the hands of people.

The Danger of Justice That Is Dehumanized

Justice runs the risk of becoming robotic and emotionless when robots are given the last say. For example, *based on past data, a sentencing algorithm can suggest more severe punishments for some groups, thereby reinforcing the prejudices it was designed to eradicate.*

Under the pretence of efficiency, such systems could perpetuate systemic unfairness in the absence of human intervention. Therefore, in automated legal systems, ethical boundaries act as safeguards against the degradation of human dignity.

The Function of Humans in a Machine Age

AI will ultimately serve to supplement human intelligence in the judiciary, not to replace it. *Although machines are faster than humans in processing information, they are unable to understand justice as a moral endeavour based on context, fairness, and empathy.* The unchanging reality is that human judgment is necessary; *an algorithm cannot replace human judgment.* Societies must keep in mind that justice is about conscience, compassion, and decision rather than just laws and statistics when establishing the ethical bounds of AI in law. Humanity must win out when machines are incapable of making decisions.

Thus, some areas of law are intrinsically moral rather than just procedural:

- **Mercy and Sentencing**: assessing the likelihood of rehabilitation and regret.
- **Family Law:** taking into account complex aspects in divorce or custody.
- **Constitutional Interpretation**: striking a balance between conflicting fundamental rights.

In some areas, AI can help with decision-making but cannot take the place of human judgment. Living experience, empathy, and moral judgment are all inherently human.

6.6. Ethical and Regulatory Guidelines

International organizations are starting to enshrine moral principles for AI in legislation:

- **The European Union AI Act (2024)**: Requires openness, auditability, and human oversight, classifying judicial AI systems as high-risk.
- **OECD AI Principles**: Advance human-centered AI, accountability, and fairness.
- **The 2021 UNESCO Recommendation on AI Ethics**: Places a strong emphasis on human rights, justice, and equity in algorithmic decision-making.
  The idea that AI should supplement human judgment rather than replace it unites these approaches.

Case Study: The Netherlands' Hybrid Human-AI Sentencing

AI-assisted sentencing for small drug offenses was tested in a pilot project in the Netherlands. AI recommendations, risk assessments, and options for rehabilitation were sent to judges. Results revealed:

- Judges' differences decreased as consistency increased.
- As AI pointed out contradictions in earlier decisions, bias declined.
- Because judges might disregard recommendations based on context or moral considerations, human judgment remained crucial.

The ethical balance is demonstrated by this hybrid paradigm, which uses people as moral judges and technology as counsellors.

6.7. Moving Towards Ethical Algorithm Design

The future of justice hinges on how responsibly these algorithms are created as artificial intelligence gets more and more integrated into judicial institutions. Transitioning from purely technical optimization to a values-driven strategy, where each phase of development—*data collection, coding, testing, and deployment*—is influenced by moral and legal considerations, is necessary to move toward ethical algorithm design.

Developers and legislators must first define what "justice," "fairness," and "accountability" imply within a particular legal and cultural environment in order to construct ethical algorithms.

This transparency guarantees that AI actively supports egalitarian outcomes rather than merely mirroring current arrangements.

The following are important foundations of ethical design:

- **Value Alignment:** Making sure AI systems uphold human rights, democratic principles, and judicial integrity.
- **Data Ethics**: use representative datasets with less bias.
- **Algorithmic Openness**, which makes auditability and explainability possible.
- **Fair Data Practices:** To stop algorithmic prejudice, use inclusive, transparent, and bias-checked datasets.
- **Explainable Logic**: Developing models that are able to explain their logic so that the public and legal experts can examine them.
- **Human Oversight:** Ensuring that machines continue to be subservient to moral reasoning by including human judgment throughout crucial decision points.
- **Continuous Evaluation:** As laws, customs, and technological advancements change, ethical audits and updates are

implemented.

In the end, integrating morality into machine intelligence is what ethical algorithm design is all about. To guarantee that AI not only complies with the law but also reflects its spirit, attorneys, ethicists, engineers, and legislators must collaborate.

By doing this, society can build systems that are not only clever but also justly intelligent, where the moral basis of human justice is strengthened rather than replaced by automation.

The ultimate objective is cognitive collaboration, a system in which humans uphold justice, empathy, and moral responsibility while AI improves efficiency, consistency, and access.

Conclusion: Moral Instruments in Machines

AI has the potential to completely transform the legal field by automating repetitive processes, increasing productivity, and offering predictive insights. However, it cannot and ought not to take the role of human conscience. In algorithmic law, ethics is the safeguard that upholds justice itself; it is not a choice.

AI's moral boundaries are obvious: although robots are capable of analysis, prediction, and advice, humans are still the moral designers of the law. The goal is to create technologies that support ethical judgment instead of outsourcing it as AI becomes more integrated into courts and legal institutions.

The role of AI in contract analysis will be discussed in the upcoming chapter, "The Age of Smart Legal Agreements," wherein human lawyers continue to be accountable for intent, fairness, and enforceability as machines read complex agreements.

Chapter 7: Contract Analysis: The Era of Intelligent Legal Contracts

Overview: Paper to Pixels

Contracts are essential to business. They protect rights, assign risk, and formalize duties. Legal experts have relied on *careful examination, negotiation, and interpretation of these documents for centuries*—often painstakingly, line by line. This method has been completely transformed by the development of artificial intelligence.

Complex agreements may now be read, compared, and interpreted by AI-driven contract analysis tools at speeds that are unthinkable for human attorneys. This change ushers in the era of smart legal agreements, a revolutionary period in which humans maintain ultimate control over intent and enforceability while machines become collaborators in legal interpretation.

7.1. AI Contract Analysis Mechanisms

Natural Language Processing (NLP), Machine Learning, and increasingly Knowledge Graphs are the main components of AI-powered contract analysis. With the use of these technologies, systems can:

- Extract important clauses (such as non-compete agreements, termination rights, and indemnities).
- Examine agreements in light of prior contracts or legal requirements.
- Point out any irregularities, contradictions, or missing clauses.
- Forecast possible dangers or vulnerability to lawsuit.

Modern AI recognizes context, in contrast to keyword search. For instance, it can emphasize minute but significant distinctions between a generic "termination clause" and one that activates under certain regulatory circumstances.

One of the most revolutionary uses of AI in the legal sector is *contract analysis*. Contract evaluation, drafting, and interpretation have historically been among the most time-consuming and prone to mistakes in legal work. *By automating the laborious, data-intensive parts of contract analysis, AI completely alters this paradigm and frees up attorneys to concentrate on strategy, negotiation, and risk management.*

Let's examine the workings of this.

7.1.1. Pre-processing and Data Intake

Large volumes of contracts, frequently in different formats like Word documents, PDFs, or scanned photos, are first ingested by AI algorithms:

- **Optical Character Recognition (OCR):** Produces machine-readable text from scanned or image-based documents.

- **Text Normalization**: Eliminates inconsistencies including typographical variations, encoding mistakes, and formatting problems.
- **Segmentation:** To prepare for focused analysis, the AI system recognizes different contract sections, such as clauses, appendices, and recitals.

In essence, the goal of this stage is to educate the AI to "read" like a lawyer, comprehending not just words but also their structure and intent.

7.1.2. **NLP, Or Natural Language Processing**

Natural Language Processing methods are used once the text has been cleaned up and organized:

- **Named Entity Recognition (NER)** recognizes important entities like dates, parties, obligations, and monetary values.
- **Reliance In order** to comprehend legal obligations, parsing maps the links between phrases ("Party A *shall indemnify* Party B").
- **Clause Classification Models** identify and label common provisions, like as confidentiality clauses, termination rights, and arbitration processes, using supervised learning.

NLP essentially transforms unstructured language into structured data so the machine can "understand" contracts on a semantic level.

7.1.3. **Clause Comparison and Machine Learning**

Machine learning algorithms that have been trained on millions of clauses form the basis of AI contract analysis:

- In comparison to industry benchmarks, supervised learning assists in determining if a clause is standard or non-standard.
- Unsupervised Learning finds trends or abnormalities in big document sets, which is useful for compliance audits or due diligence.
- Clauses from different contracts can be quickly compared using similarity scoring models to identify dangers, contradictions, or variances.

This means that long before a human lawyer would find it by hand, the AI can identify, for instance, a non-standard indemnity clause that puts a client at unnecessary risk.

7.1.4. **Compliance Analysis and Risk Scoring**

AI tools produce risk assessments for every clause or contract following the analysis stage:

- Predefined risk parameters, such as "termination for convenience," "unlimited liability," or "non-compete" prohibitions, are used to grade clauses.
- By mapping these risk scores to compliance frameworks, contracts can be made to comply with business policy, legal standards, or jurisdictional constraints.

This functionality helps businesses maintain uniformity across all contractual interactions by transforming AI into a digital compliance officer.

7.1.5. **Integration with Systems for Contract Lifecycle Management (CLM)**

In order to expedite the entire contract lifecycle, advanced AI models interface directly with business CLM platforms in addition to reviewing contracts:

- **Drafting Assistance:** AI makes clause recommendations based on prior contracts or firm templates.
- **Negotiation Insights**: It identifies the terms that are frequently disputed in comparable agreements.
- **Version Control and Audit Trails**: Compliance and supervision are seamless because each revision is recorded.

AI becomes an ongoing learning engine through integration, getting better with each contract that is examined.

7.1.6. **Ongoing Education and Model Improvement**

A feedback loop powers contemporary AI systems. The model improves its comprehension as attorneys accept, alter, or reject the system's recommendations.

- This develops organization-specific intelligence over time, adjusting to the firm's particular risk tolerance, preferred language, and drafting style.
- AI is transformed from a static instrument into an ever-improving legal partner by this learning development.

7.1.7. **Human-AI Cooperation**

Lastly, human monitoring is still crucial even when AI does the heavy labour. Attorneys understand intricate legal intricacies, authenticate AI findings, and render final judgments.

AI manages speed and scalability, while people manage context and judgment; the synergy is in increased intelligence, not replacement.

7.2 Top AI Contract Analysis Platforms

- **Systems Kira:** *Kira finds, extracts, and examines contractual provisions from thousands of documents* using machine learning. **Linklaters, Clifford Chance,** and **Deloitte** are among its clients. Kira speeds up due diligence procedures in mergers and acquisitions by cutting review times from weeks to hours by fusing AI pattern recognition with human-curated training data.
- **Luminance:** *Luminance uses unsupervised learning to identify contract risks and irregularities.* Notably, in a cross-border transaction, DLA Piper reviewed more than 200,000 papers using Luminance. Unusual clauses that could have gone overlooked were highlighted by the system, proving AI's ability to supplement human knowledge without replacing it.
- **COIN (JPMorgan)**: JPMorgan created COIN (Contract Intelligence), which automates the extraction of important contract provisions from business agreements. For example, *COIN can examine complicated credit agreements in a matter of seconds*; previously, this activity required 360,000 hours of legal labour every year. This minimizes human mistake in large-scale financial transactions while also saving time.

7.2. Integration of Blockchain and Smart Contracts

One of the most revolutionary developments in contemporary legal infrastructure is the incorporation of Blockchain technology and smart contracts into the judicial environment. When combined, they offer efficiency, immutability, and transparency, revolutionizing the way contracts are carried out and conflicts are settled.

Blockchain: The Basis of Online Credibility

Every transaction or record recorded into a blockchain is safe, transparent, and verifiable since it functions as a decentralized, tamper-proof ledger. Blockchain's immutability has the potential to transform digital identity verification, evidence management, and legal recordkeeping in the context of law and justice.

To ensure authenticity and avoid manipulation, case files, land titles, and court rulings, for instance, can be kept on blockchain networks. This promotes unparalleled confidence between courts, attorneys, and citizens by guaranteeing a single source of truth that is available to all authorized parties.

Smart Contracts: Automating Legal Responsibilities

Self-executing digital agreements stored on a blockchain are known as smart contracts. Once predetermined circumstances are met, they automatically fulfil contractual commitments without the need for middlemen. For example, in commercial law, a smart contract might initiate insurance pay-outs following event verification or immediately transfer ownership of property upon payment acceptance.

Smart contracts have the potential to reduce delays and administrative burdens in judicial settings by streamlining dispute resolution, enforcing compliance, and facilitating digital arbitration.

Increasing the Effectiveness of the Court

Courts can get automated verification, immediate execution, and tamper-proof audit trails by integrating contractual logic into blockchain platforms. By doing this, fraud, human error, and procedural manipulation are reduced. Additionally, AI-powered analytics can be integrated with smart contracts to enable predictive supervision, such as seeing high-risk transactions or possible breaches before they become disputes.

Legal and Moral Difficulties

Notwithstanding these benefits, the combination of blockchain technology and smart contracts presents important legal issues, such as:

- *How should responsibility be allocated in the event that a smart contract fails?*
- *Is it possible for code to fully convey the subtleties and intent of human agreements?*
- *In a decentralized digital transaction, which jurisdiction is applicable?*

Initiatives like the European Blockchain Services Infrastructure (EBSI), which aims to create legal guidelines for blockchain interoperability, privacy, and responsibility, are one way that EU regulators are tackling these issues. The fundamental tenet is still that automation must function inside the law, not outside of it.

A Novel Approach to Justice

The advent of algorithmic legality, a world where legal procedures are quicker, more dependable, and self-enforcing, is signalled by the combination of blockchain technology and smart contracts. However, human interpretation and supervision are still necessary in this digital paradigm to guarantee that justice maintains its moral and contextual underpinnings.

Essentially, blockchain and smart contracts are strengthening the law rather than replacing it by incorporating accuracy, transparency, and trust into the legal framework of the digital era.

Blockchain and smart contracts are becoming more and more integrated with AI-driven contract analysis. Contract terms are digitally encoded in these systems, and when conditions are met, activities are automatically carried out.

Case Study: Ethereum Smart

Decentralized contract execution is made possible via Ethereum. In the context of a supply chain, for instance, a smart contract can distribute money immediately upon delivery confirmation. By analysing code for vulnerabilities, deciphering textual terms, and confirming adherence to legal requirements, AI improves these contracts.

The combination of blockchain with AI portends a future in which contracts will be automatically executed, assessed more quickly, and continuously monitored for performance and risk.

Case Study: AI in Due Diligence for M&A

An international law firm used Kira and Luminance to examine 50,000 contracts across several jurisdictions for a significant cross-border transaction in 2022. The AI systems were able to extract important clauses in a matter of hours:

- Recommended uniformity to lower legal risk; highlighted possible compliance difficulties.

The human team then demonstrated the optimal human-AI synergy by concentrating on strategic interpretation and negotiation:

- Humans manage judgment,
- context, and intent;

AI manages scale and pattern detection.

7.3. Risk Evaluation and Litigation Forecast

The use of artificial intelligence (AI) in risk assessment and litigation forecasting signifies a paradigm change in the way businesses, legal professionals, and judicial systems predict and handle legal consequences. AI can evaluate legal risks remarkably accurately by utilizing predictive analytics, data mining, and natural language processing, assisting stakeholders in making well-informed decisions well in advance of court cases.

Predictive Legal Analytics

AI-powered predictive models examine large datasets, such as previous rulings, court documents, and legal precedents, to find trends that are associated with particular results. These systems are able to predict possible settlement ranges, projected damages, and the probability of winning a lawsuit. For instance, statistical models are used by programs like Lex Machina and Premonition AI to determine whether arguments, courts, or judges are most suited for a particular case. Through early dispute resolution methods, these technologies are being investigated more and more in the EU to enhance judicial planning, optimize workloads, and lower case backlogs.

Assessment of Risk in Legal Strategy

AI turns risk management into a data-driven science for businesses and legal firms. Legal teams can take proactive rather than reactive action by using algorithms to assess potential weaknesses in contracts, compliance requirements, or regulatory risk. AI, for example, can identify patterns of possible fraud or contractual failure in the financial services industry before they happen, allowing businesses to reduce risk by taking proactive legal action.

Forecasting Litigation in Judicial Systems

Litigation forecasting can help courts allocate resources and formulate policies at the judicial level. AI can forecast spikes in particular case categories, such as consumer protection, data privacy, or environmental litigation, by examining past data. This enables improved planning and allocation of judicial resources. Additionally, by pointing out structural inefficiencies or new legal tendencies, these insights might direct legislative improvements.

Procedural and Ethical Protections

Predictive justice presents significant ethical and legal issues despite its usefulness. If forecasts are used to prejudge cases or affect punishment, an excessive reliance on statistical probability may compromise judicial impartiality. Predictive tools must continue to be advising rather than decisive, according to the EU AI Act and the Council of Europe's Ethical Charter on the Use of AI in Judicial Systems. In order to ensure that predictions inform rather than dictate events, human judges must maintain complete discretion.

Moving Towards Knowledgeable Justice

By exposing hidden biases, standardizing interpretations, and encouraging consistency in decision-making, AI-based risk assessment and lawsuit forecasts can improve justice and transparency when used responsibly. They provide the court with a strategic lens, making it possible to manage the complexity of contemporary legal systems with greater foresight, efficiency, and readiness.

All things considered, *risk assessment and lawsuit forecasting are prime examples of the merging of data science and jurisprudence*—a future in which the law becomes predictive rather than reactive, directing society toward more intelligent, anticipatory justice.

Contractual risk can also be evaluated by contemporary AI methods. AI can identify clauses that are likely to cause issues by comparing them to databases of past litigation.

Case Study: Premonition Analytics

Premonition predicted high-risk clauses in business agreements by examining past contracts and litigation results. Premonition clients saw a roughly 30% decrease in post-signing issues, demonstrating AI's ability to avert legal disputes before they arise.

7.4. AI Contract's Ethical Considerations

At the nexus of law, automation, and morality, new ethical dilemmas arise as AI becomes more involved in the drafting, carrying out, and interpreting of contracts. While AI-generated contracts and smart contractual systems provide efficiency and accuracy, they also bring up important issues like responsibility, fairness, intent, and human oversight in digital agreements.

Accountability vs. Autonomy

With the use of blockchain integration and natural language processing, AI systems can now independently design, negotiate, and even carry out contracts. But this independence obfuscates the boundaries of legal responsibility:

- *If an AI creates a prejudiced or unenforceable clause, who is responsible?*
- *Does an AI system only copy patterns from previous data, or can it actually comprehend the parties' intentions?*

Human oversight must continue to be crucial from an ethical standpoint. Contractual AI systems that affect rights, duties, or finances are categorized as high-risk under the EU AI Act, necessitating openness, documentation, and human-in-the-loop oversight to guarantee justice and legal validity.

Discrimination and Bias

Biases ingrained in past human behaviour may be inherited by AI systems educated on historical contracts or negotiating data. This may result in unfavourable outcomes, such as duplicating discriminatory clauses or consistently benefiting one party in standardized contracts. Therefore, in order to guarantee equality in automated contracting, ethical governance requires bias checks, dataset transparency, and the capacity to explain algorithmic thinking.

Understanding and Consent

Conventional contract law depends on informed agreement and mutual understanding. However, there's a chance that one or both parties won't completely understand the implications when AI develops or implements agreements on its own. Contracts created or managed by AI must be clearly disclosed in accordance with ethical standards; parties must be aware that AI was used and have the chance to examine, alter, or reject its output prior to execution. A fundamental component of both contract law and human rights, informed consent is upheld by this principle.

Confidentiality and Data Privacy

Large amounts of commercial and personal data must be processed for AI-driven contracts. It is essential to adhere to the General Data Protection Regulation (GDPR) both legally and ethically. Strict privacy-by-design guidelines must be followed when handling sensitive data to avoid misuse, profiling, and illegal access. The system's capacity to safeguard secrecy as effectively as human attorneys is a prerequisite for trust in AI contracts.

Moral Reasoning and Human Supervision

In the end, AI is unable to understand the contextual and moral aspects of equality, good faith, or fairness. Rules can be enforced by machines, but justice cannot be interpreted by them. As a result, EU ethical standards emphasize that people must always have the last say when it comes to contract approval, enforcement, and dispute settlement. Processes may be streamlined by AI, but human judgment, empathy, and ethical reasoning must still exist.

In summary, AI contract ethics centre on striking a careful balance between utilizing automation's speed and accuracy and upholding human accountability, justice, and consent. Contracting's future rests not only on how intelligent robots get, but also on how sensibly people use them to create morally and legally good agreements.

A crucial idea is revealed: *AI is a consultant, not the ultimate judge.*

To guarantee compliance, equity, and enforceability, attorneys must validate and comprehend AI outputs.

7.5. The Human-AI Collaboration in Action

The development of justice in the digital age is reflected in the rise of human-AI collaboration in the legal and judicial environment, which combines machine intelligence with human expertise to produce quicker, more equitable, and better-informed legal decisions. Instead than taking the place of legal experts, AI acts as a co-pilot, strengthening their analytical skills and improving the accuracy and usability of legal procedures.

AI as a Helper, Not a Judge

AI functions as an intelligent helper in contemporary courtrooms and legal offices, supporting human decision-making but never taking its place. Although judges use AI technologies to summarize case law, examine precedents, and forecast potential results, the final decision is still made by a person. In order to free up time for higher-level reasoning, advocacy, and client strategy, lawyers use AI-driven platforms for contract analysis, legal research, and evidence organizing. Because of this symbiotic relationship, judicial independence and moral responsibility are strengthened rather than compromised by technology.

Collaboration in Case Management

Digital justice initiatives throughout the European Union have shown how AI and human knowledge can coexist. For example, Estonia's e-Justice system incorporates AI for document evaluation and case allocation, but judges retain complete discretion over decision-making. Similarly, although they serve only as advisory tools, France's predictive justice platforms provide data-driven insights into case trends. These examples demonstrate that efficiency and justice may coexist when humans and robots work together under ethical supervision.

Improved Assistance with Decision Making

The strength of AI is its ability to analyse enormous amounts of data at a speed that is unparalleled. AI enables legal practitioners to make more informed decisions by revealing inconsistencies, locating pertinent precedents, and highlighting potential hazards. In the meanwhile, algorithms lack the contextual, moral, and sympathetic knowledge that humans provide. As a result, the partnership produces a fair model of judgment that is both humanistic and empirical.

Transparent and Ethical Synergy

The EU's approach to human-AI cooperation is based on accountability, openness, and trust. Systems must be auditable, explainable, and comply with GDPR and EU AI Act regulations. AI outputs must be questioned, overridden, and reinterpreted by humans, who must be "in the loop." This guarantees that even when data-driven tools transform the mechanics of legal work, the integrity of justice is maintained.

Hybrid Justice's Future

The collaboration between humans and machines will grow as AI gets more advanced, able to analyse verbal clues, behavioural patterns, and legal reasoning. Hybrid judicial systems, in which AI oversees procedural efficiency while humans maintain moral rectitude and social ideals, will become more prevalent. In order to prepare the future generation of "digital judges" and "algorithmically aware lawyers," law schools and judicial academies are already adjusting, placing an emphasis on AI literacy in addition to legal doctrine.

The Human-AI partnership is essentially a reinvention of justice, in which humans uphold conscience and compassion while robots offer clarity and uniformity. Together, they create a strong coalition that guarantees the judicial system will always be both very human and technologically sophisticated.

A hybrid model is the most successful way to use AI in contract analysis:

- *Machines manage scale* by swiftly reviewing thousands of contracts, identifying trends, and highlighting possible problems.
- *Humans make decisions* about enforceability, negotiate terms, and interpret context.

The legal profession is changing as a result of this collaboration. Senior attorneys can concentrate on strategy, negotiation, and client advisory roles while junior associates are relieved of monotonous duties.

7.6. Cognitive Contracting: The Future

Cognitive contracting, a system where AI not only analyses but also recommends ideal terms, forecasts results, and combines with smart contract execution, is the next frontier. Consider an AI that can:

- Create a draft merger agreement based on previous transactions.
- Clauses that have previously resulted in legal action.
- Model various bargaining situations.
- Use a direct blockchain interface for automated execution.

In this scenario, humans give oversight, intent, and moral judgment, while AI becomes a co-author and co-strategist.

Conclusion: AI as a Co-Author of Contracts

The transition from manual review to machine-driven precision is represented by AI contract analysis. *AI systems can now comprehend, compare, and optimize contracts more quickly and correctly than ever before* thanks to OCR, NLP, machine learning, and constant feedback. *This technology is reinventing what it means to "read between the lines" in the courtroom, boardroom, or negotiation table, transforming contracts from static legal documents into dynamic, data-driven tools of strategic insight.*

Notably, one of the most obvious instances of the convergence of technology and law is the use of AI in contract analysis. It is a prime example of the equilibrium that underpins all AI in law: *humans uphold responsibility, justice, and moral reasoning while robots increase efficiency and understanding.*

Smart legal agreements represent a philosophical change in the practice, negotiation, and enforcement of the law rather than merely a technical development. They show that *AI will improve rather than replace the legal profession in the future,* with humans and machines working together to create agreements that are quicker, safer, and more accurate.

With notable examples like *Lex Machina, ROSS Intelligence, and International Legal Research Platforms*, the upcoming chapter will examine Legal Research Automation – From Books to Bots and how AI is revolutionizing the heart of legal scholarship and evidence discovery.

Chapter 8: Automation of Legal Research: From Books to Bots

Overview: The Development of Legal Studies

Legal study has been the foundation of academia, advocacy, and judicial reasoning for millennia. Attorneys carefully cross-referenced precedents and extracted principles from a plethora of case reports, legislation, and legal periodicals. The procedure was time-consuming, labour-intensive, and prone to human error.

Artificial intelligence is currently transforming this fundamental area of law. Books and paper records are giving way to *intelligent systems that can comprehend, evaluate, and forecast legal outcomes.* AI significantly speeds up and improves the accuracy of legal discovery by not just retrieving material but also interpreting context, seeing patterns, and suggesting tactics.

8.1. From Cognitive Legal Research to Keyword Search

Early digital tools made it easier to obtain statutes and case law by providing keyword search and document retrieval. Legal database pioneers LexisNexis and Westlaw revolutionized research, but they were still constrained by *syntactic search*, requiring users to manually filter results and guess the right phrases.

Semantic and cognitive search are introduced by AI. Systems like IBM Watson-based *ROSS Intelligence* are able to comprehend legal issues in natural language, decipher their meaning, and retrieve pertinent statutes, case law, and regulations. Attorneys may inquire:

"*What is the precedent for breach of contract where a delay in performance was caused by third-party interference?*"

AI systems are able to process the query, evaluate thousands of rulings, and display results that are prioritized, emphasizing arguments and possible rebuttals that could have gone unnoticed.

8.2. Top AI Legal Research Platforms

- **Lex Machina:** Legal research is converted into actionable intelligence by Lex Machina using data analytics. It forecasts litigation patterns, identifies high-risk arguments, and helps law firms design strategies by examining case outcomes, judges, and counsel performance.

Case Study: Patent Litigation in the U.S.

Lex Machina was hired by a large legal firm to evaluate the likelihood of patent infringement lawsuits. The methodology forecasted which defense tactics had a track record of success and which judges were more likely to rule in favour of plaintiffs. The AI-assisted strategy shortened preparation time and improved the company's capacity to foresee counterarguments.

- **ROSS Intelligence**: Natural language processing is used by ROSS Intelligence to comprehend legal queries and find pertinent case law. It can effectively function as a junior associate with remarkable recall and processing speed for bankruptcy law, for instance, by analysing previous decisions, identifying subtle interpretations of statutes, and even proposing alternative legal reasons.
- **CARA AI / CaseText**: CARA AI is a technology provided by CaseText that examines legal pleadings and finds pertinent authority that might have been left out. CARA AI highlights citations that support claims or reveal weaknesses by cross-referencing provided documents' linguistic content with millions of examples.

Case Study: Using AI to Find Evidence

Beyond precedents, legal research includes document review, which is essential for both regulatory compliance and litigation.

Example: eDiscovery in Class Action Lawsuits

Examining more than 5 million emails for signs of regulatory non-compliance was a difficulty for a multinational corporation. The company marked high-priority documents, classified them according to relevancy, and automated the initial assessment using AI-powered technologies. After then, human attorneys concentrated on reasoning and analysis.

The outcome shows how AI improves research and operational efficiency in legal practice, with a 70% reduction in review time and much lower expenses.

8.3. Legal Predictive Analytics

AI is capable of predicting legal developments in addition to retrieval. By connecting judges, courts, and past results, platforms such as Lex Machina and Premonition offer *predictive analytics*. Attorneys are able to predict opposing arguments, assess the likelihood of victory for certain claims, and develop tactics based on previous facts.

Case Study: Conflict in Employment Law

> Predictive analytics was utilized by a law firm preparing for a wrongful termination lawsuit to determine whether a settlement or trial was more likely. AI examined previous decisions in the area, taking into account the claim's nature, the judge's background, and comparable precedents. The negotiation strategy was guided by this data-driven insight, which maximized positive results while lowering risk.

8.4. International Application: AI in Legal Research

- **USA:** Corporate law firms are dominated by AI platforms, particularly when it comes to intellectual property, commercial litigation, and regulatory compliance.
- **United Kingdom:** Businesses use AI in conjunction with cloud-based practice management to help with contract analysis, compliance, and case preparation.
- **Europe:** AI-assisted case outcome predictions is emphasized by legal research portals like Predictice in France.
- **Africa:** New projects in Kenya, South Africa, and Nigeria use AI for research, document processing, and case management to aid with backlogs and scarce legal resources.

These illustrations show that AI in legal research may democratize access to justice everywhere, *not just in developed countries.*

8.5. Ethical Issues in AI Legal Research

Important ethical concerns are raised by AI in legal research:

1. **Accuracy and Reliability:** Systems need to be verified to make sure they deliver accurate and pertinent information. Legal strategy could be misguided by incorrect outputs.
2. **Transparency:** Attorneys need to comprehend how AI makes suggestions. Professional accountability is compromised by blind reliance.
3. **Bias:** Systemic biases found in earlier decisions may be replicated by AI educated on historical data. To stop injustice from continuing, vigilance is required.
4. **Client Confidentiality**: To safeguard private legal papers when utilizing cloud-based AI solutions, strong security is necessary.

The primary idea is straightforward: human judgment is still the final arbitrator of legal reasoning, and *AI is an addition rather than a substitute.*

8.6. Revolutionizing Legal Education

Legal education is changing as a result of the development of AI research tools. The following are currently taught to law students:

- *How to formulate natural language legal questions for AI systems.*
- *How to critically assess outcomes produced by AI.*
- *How litigation strategy can use predictive analytics.*

Future attorneys will be proficient in both law and artificial intelligence, enabling them to work well with intelligent technologies.

8.7. Legal Research's Future

Reactive retrieval will give way to *proactive legal advice* in the next generation of AI:

- *By examining cases, laws, and trends, AI will create strategic briefs.*
- *Complex legal relationships across jurisdictions will be mapped using integrated knowledge graphs.*
- *AI might offer guidance on regulatory compliance, settlement choices, and risk score for legal disputes.*

Lawyers will be able to concentrate on high-level interpretation, advocacy, and judgment as legal research transforms from a manual information-gathering process to a strategic decision-support system.

Conclusion: From Books to Bots

Automation of legal research is a significant change in the legal profession. *AI solutions improve speed, accuracy, and strategic decision-making by converting unprocessed data into actionable insight.*

However, human judgment is still crucial, just like with any AI in law. While machines are capable of retrieval, analysis, and prediction, human intelligence is necessary for policy evaluation, legal interpretation, and discretion.

Legal research is no longer limited to libraries; it is now a cooperative effort between intelligent algorithms and human attorneys, paving the way for a quicker, more accurate, and more approachable legal practice.

Contract Analysis Revisited: AI and Smart Legal Drafting will be covered in the following chapter. Building on research automation, it will look at how AI co-authors contracts, forecasts risk, and guarantees compliance.

Chapter 9: A Review of Contract Analysis AI and Intelligent Legal Drafting

Overview: Beyond Evaluation to Production

AI-assisted legal drafting is the current frontier, whereas Chapter 7 examined AI in contract analysis—extracting clauses, evaluating risk, and identifying anomalies. AI shifts from passive review to active co-creation, creating, refining, and forecasting the legal and commercial ramifications of contractual wording in smart legal drafting.

There are significant ramifications. *Attorneys are becoming more than just document interpreters; they are strategic supervisors who help AI create legally binding, equitable, and contextually relevant agreements at previously unheard-of speeds.*

9.1. AI as a Co-Author

By evaluating millions of previous contracts, identifying best practices, and recommending standard terms, AI systems now aid in contract drafting. AI, in contrast to human drafters, can quickly analyse hundreds of previous contracts to foresee possible ambiguities, disagreements, or lawsuit threats.

Important Platforms

- **Kira Systems:** By identifying possible hazards based on previous occurrences, Kira can provide optimum phrasing for complex agreements in addition to clause extraction.
- **Luminance:** Makes use of unsupervised learning to identify odd clauses, make modification suggestions, and advise portfolio standardization.
- **ClauseIQ** and **ThoughtRiver:** These tools assess clauses in context, highlighting phrasing that can raise regulatory or compliance issues and offering substitutes based on prior legal decisions.

Case Study: Drafting for Cross-Border M&A

A law firm used Kira and Luminance to design and align contracts across three jurisdictions in an international merger in 2023. AI reduced the amount of time needed for manual drafting by 65% by suggesting substitute phrases that were compliant with local laws and regulations. The *human-AI drafting relationship* was demonstrated by human lawyers who concentrated on negotiation, risk assessment, and strategic customization.

9.2. Risk Prediction and Predictive Drafting

Through risk prediction and predictive drafting, two technologies that are revolutionizing the analysis, creation, and management of contracts, artificial intelligence is completely changing the legal environment. In order to foresee future legal issues and produce optimal contract wording before disputes even emerge, these systems employ sophisticated machine learning and natural language processing (NLP).

In order to find patterns of failure or conflict, risk prediction entails training AI models on big legal datasets, such as previous contracts, litigation results, and regulatory histories. For instance, *an AI tool can identify unclear wording that could lead to future disputes, identify clauses that have historically resulted in litigation, or evaluate compliance weaknesses in a draft agreement.* Lawyers and businesses can reduce legal exposure far in advance of signing thanks to this proactive capabilities, which saves time and money.

Conversely, predictive drawing goes beyond automation. Using predictive text creation, *AI-driven systems can create personalized contracts with terms that are tailored to the risk profile, industry, and jurisdiction.* By combining best practices, precedent research, and changing legal norms, these technologies not only speed up the drafting of documents but also improve their quality.

Risk prediction and predictive drafting together signify a change in legal practice from reactive to preventive—from handling issues after they arise to creating contracts that reduce them. But the ethical aspect is still crucial: *human moral judgment and legal judgment cannot be replaced by predictive algorithms.* Attorneys must continue to be the last arbiters of fairness, context, and intent.

In the digital age, these technologies essentially redefine legal artistry, with AI-powered foresight serving as the new cornerstone of justice and contractual integrity.

Contract performance and possible disagreements are now predicted by AI systems. AI can identify terms that have previously resulted in legal action or regulatory issues by examining historical data.

For instance, *employment contracts*: A company utilized AI to design non-compete agreements, examining previous court decisions to suggest wording that struck a balance between enforceability and equity. AI anticipated possible sites of judicial scrutiny, enabling attorneys to proactively modify text to reduce risk.

This *predictive capacity combines legal accuracy with useful foresight* to guarantee that contracts are both strategically sound and syntactically correct.

9.3. Automated Execution and Smart Contracts

The emergence of smart contracts and automated execution signifies a major change in the creation, implementation, and enforcement of legal agreements. Smart contracts, which are self-executing digital agreements with terms directly inscribed into computer code, are powered by blockchain technology and artificial intelligence. Without the need for middlemen, attorneys, or courts, the contract automatically fulfils once predetermined criteria are fulfilled.

Fundamentally, smart contracts convert conventional legal responsibilities into logic that can be understood by machines. For instance, a smart contract controlling a loan may initiate repayment upon reaching predetermined milestones or release funds automatically upon confirmation of the borrower's credit. By ensuring speed, accuracy, and transparency, this technology lowers the possibility of fraud and human error.

AI improves smart contracts by allowing for intelligent and flexible execution. By evaluating risk, interpreting real-world data (via IoT integration or data oracles), and dynamically modifying contractual terms, machine learning algorithms can give legal frameworks previously unheard-of responsiveness.

But there are serious moral and legal concerns with this automation:

- *If a smart contract fails or acts unfairly, who is responsible?*
- *How should unchangeable laws that impose unfair results be handled by the legal system?*
- *Can computational logic capture moral judgment, which is crucial to justice?*

These difficulties highlight the necessity of hybrid governance solutions that blend human monitoring with technical accuracy.

In the end, smart contracts and automated execution represent the digitalization of trust. By integrating legal guarantees into technology, society advances toward a future in which the law serves as both a code and a conscience—a system in which the intelligent structures of the digital era not only write the law but also carry it out.

Blockchain-based smart contracts, which *run automatically when certain criteria are satisfied*, are becoming more and more integrated with AI drafting.

Case Study: Smart Contracting in the Supply Chain

> A multinational logistics business integrated terms into Ethereum-based smart contracts using AI-assisted supplier agreement drafting. AI confirmed that contractual obligations complied with local law and could be read by machines.
>
> Payments were made automatically when delivery milestones were met, guaranteeing efficiency and compliance while lowering human error.

The *entire lifespan potential* of AI—drafting, analysis, risk assessment, and execution—is demonstrated by this combination.

9.4. Legal and Ethical Issues

While the incorporation of automation, blockchain, and artificial intelligence into legal institutions offers accuracy and efficiency, it also presents a complicated web of ethical and legal issues that question conventional ideas of accountability, justice, and responsibility. The law must change to address new issues that go beyond human precedent as smart contracts, predictive analytics, and autonomous decision-making become more commonplace.

Liability is one of the main issues:

- *Who is held accountable when an AI-driven system or smart contract makes a mistake, such as executing a defective clause or misinterpreting data?*
- *The algorithm itself, the user, or the developer?*

By incorporating semi-autonomous actors into the legal process, artificial intelligence (AI) undermines the foundation of traditional legal frameworks, which were constructed around human activity.

Algorithmic opacity, or the inability to completely comprehend how complex AI models arrive at their results, also raises ethical concerns. A fair legal system depends on the concepts of due process, explainability, and judicial review, all of which are compromised by this "black box" issue. Furthermore, biases concealed in training data may result in discriminatory outcomes that jeopardize legal equality.

Consent and fairness are issues that smart contracts bring up. Parties might not completely understand the significance of every condition buried in the code because they are automatically created and executed. Furthermore, when mistakes or injustices need to be corrected, blockchain's immutability—which is sometimes viewed as a strength—can turn into a vulnerability because conventional channels for redress might not be available.

Additionally, there are wider cultural ramifications. *AI has the potential to dehumanize justice by reducing moral and contextual judgment to computational efficiency as it takes on more responsibilities in legal reasoning and enforcement.* Therefore, ethical governance must make sure that technology enhances human conscience and legal reasoning rather than substitutes them.

Thus, strong legal protections and moral precepts must direct the way toward algorithmic justice. To guarantee accountability, openness, and the preservation of human dignity, laws must change. Only then will technology be able to fulfil its proper role as a reliable tool in the digital era, rather than as the judge of justice.

Even if AI increases productivity, moral and legal issues still exist:

1. **Responsibility:** When it comes to contractual language, humans must continue to bear ultimate responsibility. Lawyers are in charge of intent, enforceability, and compliance, even though AI may suggest provisions.
2. **Bias and Standardization**: AI that has been educated on past contracts may reinforce unfair terms that disproportionately penalize particular parties. To guarantee justice, vigilance is necessary.
3. **Confidentiality and Data Security:** AI platforms need to guarantee strong encryption and privacy safeguards because drafting frequently involves sensitive company data.
4. **Transparency and Explainability:** In order to uphold professional and ethical duty, attorneys must comprehend why AI recommends specific terminology or adjustments.

The idea is straightforward: *Humans Rule, AI Helps.*

9.5. Case Study: Banking's Hybrid Human-AI Drafting

A multinational bank standardized loan agreements across several nations by using AI-assisted drafting. AI reduced drafting time by 70% by proposing improved terms for collateral management, default remedies, and interest computation. Legal staff ensured adherence to local legislation by validating and improving the text.

The *ideal balance* (optimal balance) is demonstrated by this hybrid model, where people contextualize and take on legal obligation while AI scales and standardizes.

9.6. The Next Frontier: Cognitive Contracting

Moving beyond static smart contracts to systems that comprehend, reason, and adapt like a human legal counsel, cognitive contracting is the next frontier in legal innovation. Cognitive contracts, which are powered by sophisticated artificial intelligence and natural language processing, can decipher intricate provisions, foresee unforeseen events, and react dynamically to changing conditions, turning contracts from inflexible commitments into intelligent, living tools.

Cognitive contracts are *capable of context analysis, risk prediction, and real-time modification recommendations*, in contrast to **Traditional or Smart Contracts** that *rigidly adhere to pre-set rules.* A supply chain agreement might, for example, automatically modify delivery terms in the event of an unexpected market interruption or identify problems with regulatory compliance before they become disputes.

Contracts not only uphold duties but also maximize results and reduce disputes in this proactive and flexible legal environment.

Predictive analytics, machine learning, and legal reasoning frameworks are also integrated by cognitive contracting, allowing systems to model possible outcomes, assess different courses of action, and direct stakeholders toward the best choices. These contracts function as both strategic advisors and execution engines by fusing automation and insight.

However, new ethical and legal issues are brought forth by this evolution. As AI takes on quasi-intelligent decision-making tasks, questions of culpability, interpretability, and moral judgment grow more complicated. To keep technology from surpassing the moral underpinnings of law, regulators and legal experts must create frameworks that guarantee responsibility, transparency, and harmony with human values.

The distinction between autonomous legal reasoning systems and legal instruments will become hazier as a result of cognitive contracting, which essentially portends a time when contracts will be intelligent, responsive, and ethically led entities rather than static artefacts. In addition to efficiency, this frontier promises to rethink how the legal system can operate in the digital era.

Cognitive contracting is emerging from AI-assisted drafting:

- **Dynamic Clause Suggestion**: AI suggests clauses that adjust to changes in industry, jurisdiction, and regulations.
- **Scenario Simulation**: Using predictive modelling, attorneys can assess how contract language might function in the event of fictitious conflicts or changes in the market.
- **Continuous Compliance Monitoring:** AI keeps track of corporate policy changes, regulatory updates, and amendments, automatically recommending modifications to ensure legal compliance.

By continuously learning and refining contractual language, AI effectively turns into an *Intelligent Collaborator* that minimizes legal exposure, improves fairness, and reduces ambiguity.

9.7. AI Drafting's Human Role

The human role is still crucial even as artificial intelligence uses automation, predictive analytics, and cognitive contracting to transform contract drafting. *AI is capable of producing language, suggesting sentences, and identifying hazards, but it is unable to mimic the ethical reasoning, judgment, or intuition that form the foundation of successful legal practice.*

AI is unable to fully comprehend the contextual understanding that humans bring, which includes knowledge of company goals, cultural quirks, and strategic priorities. They make sure that the terms of the contract are in line with the parties' intentions, legal requirements, and moral principles. Additionally, attorneys act as crucial supervisors, deciphering AI results, clarifying misunderstandings, and rendering judgments in circumstances where machine logic can be inadequate or unduly strict.

Another important human duty is ethical supervision. AI systems that have been trained on past data may unintentionally spread unfair clauses, bias, or legal mistakes. In order to ensure justice, accountability, and conformity to social standards, human attorneys must critically assess these recommendations.

In the end, AI in writing should be seen as a cooperative collaborator rather than a substitute. Legal professionals can concentrate on strategic thinking, negotiation, and judgment-intensive duties since it speeds up procedures, improves accuracy, and minimizes repeated work.

In summary, the future of legal writing will be hybrid, with humans contributing wisdom, ethics, and accountability and AI handling efficiency and pattern recognition to produce contracts that are both technically accurate and morally decent.

Despite AI's capabilities, humans are still essential for:

- *Determining purpose and business strategy;*
- *Negotiating complicated agreements;*
- *Ensuring ethical and legal compliance; and*
- *Interpreting unclear or ethically delicate provisions.*

AI is a tool for accuracy, insight, and efficiency, not a substitute for human judgment.

Conclusion: AI as a Strategic Partner in Drafting

The revolutionary synergy between AI and human skill is exemplified by smart legal drafting:

- Humans offer judgment, context, and ethical oversight;
- AI increases speed, consistency, and predictive capacity;
- Together, they produce contracts that are effective, compliant, and strategically sound.

This chapter shows that AI in law is a co-author, analyst, and risk advisor rather than a replacement for the lawyer's trade. This allows lawyers to concentrate on strategy and judgment while delegating repetitive or data-intensive duties to intelligent systems.

Predictive Judgments — AI in Decision Forecasting and Sentencing will be examined in the following chapter, along with the ethical limits of algorithmic foresight and systems that predict court decisions.

Chapter 10: AI in Decision Forecasting and Sentencing via Predictive Judgments

Overview: Predicting Justice

Law, precedent, and discretion have always been balanced in judicial decision-making. Before making decisions, judges assess the influence on society, evaluate the evidence, and interpret the law. Predictive Judgments—*tools that examine enormous legal datasets to predict outcomes, assess risk, and guide sentencing*—are one way artificial intelligence is currently entering this process.

Predictive systems offer data-driven insight rather than taking the place of judicial discretion. They have huge potential to improve efficiency, decrease bias, and increase consistency. However, they also bring up important moral and legal issues, such as accountability, openness, and justice.

10.1. How Predictive Judgments Work

One of the most sophisticated uses of AI in the legal system is **Predictive Judgments**, *which enable courts, attorneys, and organizations to predict court outcomes using algorithmic modelling and historical data*. In order to find patterns and correlations that can predict future decisions in new cases, predictive judgment systems fundamentally examine enormous archives of previous cases, rulings, statutes, and legal opinion.

Usually, the procedure entails the following crucial steps:

1. **Data Collection and Preparation**: *Court rulings, case files, precedents, and regulatory texts are among the structured and unstructured legal data that AI systems collect*. Data is cleansed, sorted, and converted into machine learning-ready formats.
2. **Pattern Recognition and Modelling**: *Recurring elements linked to case outcomes are found by machine learning algorithms*, which frequently use natural language processing (NLP). Jurisdiction, legal arguments, judge conduct, and precedent significance are a few examples.
3. **Probability Assessment:** The *AI gives possible outcomes, including whether a motion will be granted or a case will settle, a likelihood*. These forecasts offer guidance rather than absolute certainty since they are probabilistic rather than deterministic.
4. **Decision Support:** Attorneys *utilize predictive insights to guide strategy* in areas including lawsuit risk assessment, settlement negotiations, and argument drafting that follow trends identified by the system.
5. **Continuous Learning:** By adding new cases and results over time, predictive judgment models get better and may adjust to changing legal norms and trends.

While predictive judgments offer **efficiency and foresight**, they raise critical concerns about **bias, transparency, and overreliance**. AI predictions are only as unbiased as the data they are trained on, and human oversight is essential to ensure fairness and uphold the principles of justice.

In essence, predictive judgments function as a **decision-support tool**, augmenting human legal reasoning with data-driven foresight, enabling more informed, strategic, and proactive legal practice.

Natural language processing, machine learning, and historical legal data are the foundations of predictive judging systems. These systems examine the following:

- *Legal arguments and case features;*
- *Judicial tendencies and rulings;*
- *Socioeconomic and demographic data (where ethically permitted); and*
- *Previous case results.*

AI can determine the likelihood of conviction or acquittal, the likelihood that an appeal would be successful, and appropriate punishment ranges by modelling trends in previous rulings.

Case Study: COMPAS Risk Assessment Tool

> Several U.S. jurisdictions use COMPAS, which forecasts recidivism risk, to guide sentencing and parole choices. Although contentious, it shows how AI can supplement court rulings by offering organized, data-driven insights rather than taking the place of human judgment.

10.2. International Applications

10.2.1. The United States:

- **Sentencing Algorithms**: Defendants receive risk assessments from programs like COMPAS and PSA (Public Safety Assessment).
- **Predictive Analytics in Appeals:** To predict likely outcomes, Lex Machina examines previous appellate rulings.

10.2.2. China:

- **Smart Court Systems:** AI-assisted courts emphasize legal precedents, summarize evidence, and provide preliminary rulings for judges to consider.

10.2.3. United Kingdom:

- In an effort to standardize sentencing and lessen disparities between jurisdictions, pilot programs investigate AI-assisted sentencing in minor criminal cases.

10.2.4. Europe :

- **Predictive Case Management:** To help with court assignments, resource allocation, and case prioritizing, platforms examine litigation trends.

These applications demonstrate the range of predictive AI in the legal field, from semi-autonomous decision-making support to advisory aids.

Case Study: Dutch Predictive Sentencing

AI was used in a trial study in the Netherlands to predict sentencing results for non-violent drug offenses. The AI examined the following: the defendant's past; the specifics of the crime; and earlier court rulings

The findings showed less variation in punishment, encouraging uniformity and equity. Nonetheless, judges maintained the authority to reject AI recommendations, highlighting the human-centered methodology necessary for moral implementation.

10.3. Moral Aspects

Predictive assessments present urgent moral dilemmas:

1. **Discrimination and Bias**

- Certain demographics may be disproportionately impacted by AI's inheritance of prior biases in court data.
- Diverse, representative datasets and ongoing auditing are necessary for mitigation.

2. **Transparency**

- The right to know how predictive scores affect sentencing is granted to defendants.
- Due process may be compromised by black-box algorithms.

3. **Accountability**

- Should a defendant receive a sentence based on AI guidance, who bears the blame for mistakes—*the institution, the AI developer, or the judge?*

4. **Privacy and Data Protection**

- Systems must adhere to legal requirements like GDPR and handle sensitive personal data in an ethical manner.

Case Study: Loomis v. State (2016)

The U.S. Supreme Court considered whether applying COMPAS risk assessments to sentencing violated constitutional rights in the Wisconsin case. The Court stressed the *importance of human judgment* and the necessity of accountability and openness while permitting the use of AI for advising purposes.

10.4. Legal Strategy and Predictive Analytics

Additionally, predictive technologies help attorneys by assessing the following:

- *Probability of litigation success;*
- *Best-case or worst-case settlement ranges;*
- *Judges' and the court's inclinations;*
- *Opposing counsel's tactics.*

For instance, in order to maximize case strategy, patent litigation forecasting firms employ Lex Machina to predict whether judges will favour plaintiffs or defendants. This strategy lowers uncertainty, directs the distribution of resources, and enhances customer results.

10.5. AI's Boundaries for Judicial Forecasting

Predictive AI has limits even though it can improve decision-making:

- **Interpretability:** AI is capable of displaying probabilities, but it is unable to elucidate complex logic or ethical issues.
- **Dynamic Legal Context**: As the law changes, new statutes, precedents, and social norms may not be reflected in historical data.
- **Moral Judgment**: Discretion, kindness, and proportionality are aspects of sentencing that machines cannot imitate.
- **Principle:** AI should support human judgment in all legal decisions, not take its place.

10.6. Hybrid Judicial Decision Support: The Future

Hybrid models will be the main emphasis of the upcoming generation of AI in forecasting and sentencing:

- AI creates risk assessments by analysing past data and spotting trends.
- When interpreting AI output, human judges take sociological, ethical, and moral considerations into account.
- Constant observation guarantees accountability, openness, and justice.

This strategy makes use of AI's capabilities for size, consistency, and data understanding while maintaining *judicial discretion*.

10.7. Case Study: AI in Juvenile Justice in the U.S.

AI-assisted juvenile justice systems are now being tested in a few jurisdictions:

- AI forecasts rehabilitation potential and recidivism risk.
- Instead of imposing harsh penalties, judges utilize these forecasts to provide tailored solutions.

This demonstrates how AI can *assist restorative justice strategies* in addition to *predicting results.*

Conclusion: Forecasting Carefully

With its efficiency, uniformity, and data-driven understanding, predictive judgments represent a paradigm shift in legal practice. However, they also draw attention to *algorithmic law's practical and ethical limitations.*

AI can *predict results, identify patterns, and direct decision-making, but moral judgment, discretion, and accountability are still the domain of humans.*

The Digital Bench and the Future of Advocacy, the upcoming chapter on AI in Courtrooms, will look at how AI technologies interact with judges, attorneys, and litigants in the real-time legal setting.

Chapter 11: AI in Courtrooms - Advocacy's Future and the Digital Bench

Overview: The Digital Age Arrives in the Courtroom

The conventional courtroom, which is a setting for discussion, testimony, and verdict, is drastically changing. Artificial intelligence is becoming more *prevalent in the courtroom itself*, supporting judges, attorneys, and litigants. It is no longer just used for contract evaluation or behind-the-scenes research.

The *digital bench* transforms advocacy, strategy, and access to justice with AI-assisted evidence presentation and predictive insights on decisions. This chapter investigates the use of AI in real-time courtroom procedures, looking at practical applications, ethical issues, and worldwide implementations.

As digital technology become ingrained in judicial systems across the globe, the modern courtroom is undergoing a significant transition. *An environment that was formerly characterized by paper records, tangible proof, and manual processes is now changing into one that is highly linked and data-driven.* The administration of justice is changing as a result of artificial intelligence, cloud-based case management systems, digital evidence platforms, and remote hearing capabilities.

This change signifies a structural evolution in legal procedures rather than just a technology advancement. Through real-time data tracing and auditability, digital tools are strengthening transparency, speeding up case resolution, and enhancing access to justice. AI-powered research engines, automated transcribing tools, and predictive analytics that support legal strategy are just a few examples of how technology is making court operations quicker, more accurate, and more effective.

However, *there are difficulties with the change*. In the digital age, courts must manage concerns about cybersecurity, data integrity, algorithmic bias, justice, and the preservation of human judgment. The objective is to improve the ability of judges and attorneys rather than to replace them, making sure that technology upholds ethical standards and constitutional principles.

Justice is becoming more accessible, accountable, and intelligent as the digital era enters the courtroom, paving the way for a time when strong, transparent, and human-centered technologies will enhance legal decision-making.

11.1. AI's Mechanisms in Courts

Judicial systems are progressively incorporating artificial intelligence to supplement human decision-making rather than to replace it. AI functions in courts through a number of crucial mechanisms:

1. **Predictive Analytics**

AI is capable of analyzing past case data to spot trends and predict probable outcomes. These insights are used by judges and attorneys to guide strategy, evaluate risks, and expedite decision-making.

1. **Automation of Legal Research**

AI can swiftly examine statutes, case law, and legal precedents thanks to Natural Language Processing (NLP), providing pertinent information in a matter of seconds and cutting down on the time needed for manual study.

1. **Analysis of Documents and Evidence**

AI systems are capable of scanning, classifying, and summarizing vast amounts of digital evidence, contracts, and documents. They can highlight important material for judicial examination, identify abnormalities, and flag contradictions.

1. **Tools for Making Decisions**

While maintaining judicial discretion, AI-powered platforms offer judges score systems or recommendations that assist in identifying pertinent variables for sentence, bail, or civil judgments.

1. **Automated Courtroom Recording and Transcription**

AI-enabled transcription systems improve record-keeping, accessibility, and the effectiveness of post-trial evaluations by instantly converting spoken proceedings into correct text.

1. **Intelligent Case Management Systems**

AI increases court administrative efficiency by organizing caseloads, scheduling hearings, keeping track of deadlines, and ranking cases according to complexity or urgency.

1. **Risk and Fraud Identification**

In order to help avoid fraud or misconduct during court procedures, machine learning algorithms can identify abnormalities in files, financial documents, or evidentiary submissions.

Diagram: AI's Mechanism in Courts

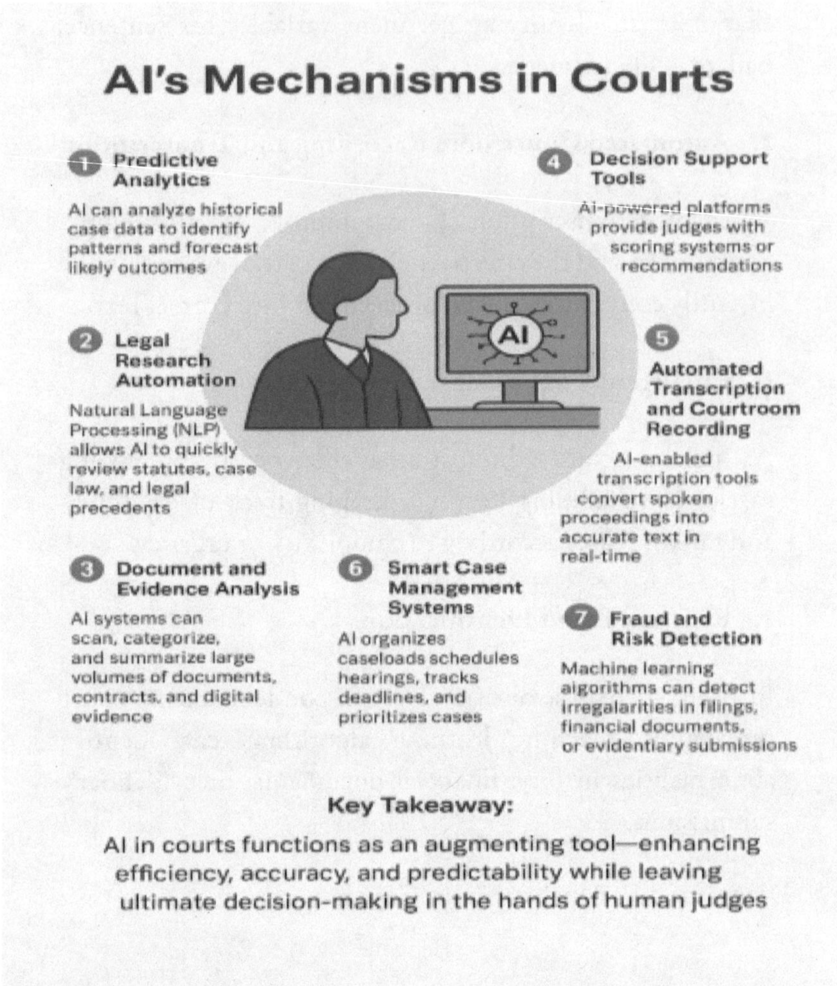

Figure 1: AI's Mechanism in Courts

AI systems used in courts usually carry out a number of tasks, including:

- **Evidence Analysis:** assessing the applicability and dependability of documents, photos, and audio/video.
- **Legal Research:** offering immediate access to case law, statutes, and precedents.

- **Decision Support**: Providing risk analyses, result probabilities, or recommended decisions.
- **Automation** of administrative tasks, such as filing, scheduling, and following procedures.

AI improves *consistency, speed, and accuracy*, freeing up human actors to concentrate on advocacy, judgment, and moral decision-making.

Key Takeaway: AI serves as an augmenting tool in courts, improving efficiency, accuracy, and predictability while leaving human judges to make the final decisions. In the digital age, its techniques allow courts to handle increasingly complicated legal environments while streamlining procedures and cutting down on delays.

11.2. International Applications

China: Intelligent Courts

When it comes to AI-assisted court systems, China is a leader. Among the noteworthy characteristics are:

- **Evidence pre-screening**: AI examines and condenses case files.
- **Preliminary Judgment Drafts**: AI creates recommendations for court review in preliminary judgment drafts.
- **Video Analytics:** Sentiment analysis and facial recognition are used to track courtroom encounters.

Case Study: Hangzhou Internet Court

The court, which specializes in e-commerce disputes, processes claims, summarizes evidence, and makes recommendations for decisions using AI. Judges still have the last say, but they rely on AI to manage a lot of cases quickly, cutting down on backlogs and delays.

Estonia: The e-Judge Pilot

Transparency and explainability are key components of Estonian judicial innovation:

- For minor disputes, AI-assisted systems offer preliminary rulings.
- Human judges review and approve recommendations, making them completely auditable.
- The technology ensures speed and accuracy by integrating with legal databases and digital evidence.

AI may *improve court efficiency* without sacrificing human oversight or accountability, as this pilot shows.

The United States and the United Kingdom

- AI tools support risk assessment, document review, and evidence management.
- By forecasting judicial trends and probable decisions, platforms like Lex Machina and Premonition inform strategy.
- Courts are still wary about using AI to make decisions, giving advisory functions precedence over independent judgment.

11.3. AI-Powered Evidence Evaluation

The term "AI-Powered Evidence Evaluation" describes the application of artificial intelligence technologies to help courts and legal professionals organize, analyze, and evaluate evidence during court hearings. AI is significantly more efficient than humans at processing vast amounts of papers, photos, videos, audio recordings, and other types of evidence, spotting pertinent patterns, contradictions, or important details.

Important Features:

1. **Automated Document Analysis:** AI can identify inconsistencies and highlight relevant information by scanning contracts, witness statements, and case files.
2. **Multimedia Evidence Processing:** AI systems can analyze audio, video, and picture evidence, spotting irregularities, confirming authenticity, or recognizing important information like faces, places, or objects.
3. **Predictive Relevance Scoring:** AI can help judges and attorneys prioritize review by ranking evidence according to how probable it is to be important to a case.
4. **Bias and Anomaly Detection:** Sophisticated AI may identify discrepancies or possible evidence manipulation, improving the evaluation of believability.
5. **Integration with Case Management Systems:** AI solutions can expedite courtroom preparation by connecting assessed evidence with case schedules, legal precedents, and procedural workflows.

Impact on Legal Practice:

- It helps judges and attorneys make better decisions by

expediting pre-trial preparation and minimizing human error.
- Raises concerns regarding openness because, in order to guarantee justice in court, the procedures of AI evaluation must be explicable.

One of the most significant uses of AI in the legal system is evidence analysis:

- **Document review**: AI draws attention to pertinent agreements, clauses, or earlier decisions.
- **Multimedia analysis**: Evidence from audio, video, and images is examined for irregularities or trends.
- **Forensic insight**: AI helps with digital forensics, authentication, and fraud detection.

Case Study: eDiscovery in High-Stakes Litigation

In a corporate fraud case, a U.S. legal firm used artificial intelligence to examine 10 million internal emails. AI significantly cut down on human review time by identifying important evidence, highlighting discrepancies, and proposing links between documents. Using these findings, judges and attorneys shifted their attention from manual review to arguments.

Thus, AI is progressively changing the evaluation and interpretation of evidence in contemporary courtrooms. Artificial intelligence (AI) systems may swiftly find important information, spot errors, and highlight any anomalies that would evade human scrutiny by examining enormous amounts of papers, multimedia files, and digital records. Beyond speed, these technologies can rank evidence's significance to a case, assess its relevance and reliability, and even compare results with prior rulings or procedural requirements. AI enhances human judgment by giving courts and attorneys a data-driven lens through which to examine complicated cases, even as it offers previously unheard-of efficiency and insight. For AI-supported assessments to improve fairness and preserve the integrity of judicial decision-making, transparency and explainability are still crucial.

11.4. Advocacy and AI: Improving Legal Argumentation

By giving attorneys the means to create more accurate, convincing, and fact-based arguments, artificial intelligence is revolutionizing the practice of legal advocacy. By analyzing previous case law, identifying pertinent statutes, and highlighting judicial reasoning patterns, *AI systems might give advocates insights that improve their written and oral presentations.* AI enables attorneys to foresee difficulties and improve their tactics by modeling counterarguments, anticipating possible judicial issues, and recommending the best way to organize points.

Crucially, although AI improves debate, it cannot take the place of human attorneys' sophisticated knowledge, moral discernment, and persuasive abilities in the courtroom. Rather, it serves as an astute collaborator, empowering advocates to make stronger, more confident, and more successful arguments.

AI isn't just for judges. AI is being used by lawyers more and more to:

- Find precedents and counterarguments.
- Forecast the strategy of the opposing counsel.
- Based on past statistics, assess probable judicial reactions.

Case Study: Forecasting Techniques in Intellectual Property Conflicts

AI analytics was utilized by a legal firm to determine which patent litigation claims were most persuasive. AI identified patterns in court thinking by analysing thousands of previous rulings. After that, attorneys created customized arguments by combining AI-driven understanding with human ingenuity.

11.5. AI Courtroom Ethics

Ethical issues in the application of artificial intelligence are crucial as it becomes a crucial component of legal procedures. In order to prevent biases that could skew court decisions, courts must make sure AI tools respect the values of impartiality, justice, and transparency. *When AI is used in evidence review, predictive analytics, or legal argumentation, human oversight is crucial because judges and attorneys are still ultimately in charge of making decisions.* Explainability is another requirement for ethical deployment; *AI systems must offer logic that is comprehensible and subject to legal scrutiny.* Additionally, as AI depends on large datasets that may contain private or sensitive information, privacy, data security, and the protection of sensitive data are crucial. AI is essentially a strong ally in the courtroom, but in order to preserve public confidence in the legal system, its advantages must be weighed against stringent ethical restrictions.

Complex ethical issues are raised by AI in courtrooms:

1. **Explainability and Transparency**: Litigants need to comprehend AI advice. Due process may be compromised by black-box systems.
2. **Bias Mitigation**: AI systems need to be routinely examined and modified because historical judicial data may include systematic bias.
3. **Accountability:** AI cannot be held legally accountable; judges still have the last say.
4. **Privacy and Confidentiality**: AI systems must guarantee adherence to ethical and legal norms because courtrooms contain sensitive data.

Principle: AI does not take the role of human judgment or moral discretion; rather, it is a tool for efficiency and understanding.

11.6. The Digital Bench: Creating Justice's Future

Important Features:

- **AI-Assisted Judgments**: Provides judges with evidence analysis and prediction insights.
- **hybrid decision-making:** For balanced results, hybrid decision-making combines human judgment with AI suggestions.
- **Digital evidence management** simplifies the examination of case data, multimedia, and documents.
- **Explainability and transparency** guarantee that AI reasoning can be examined and relied upon.
- **Improved Accessibility:** Facilitates more public access, quicker decisions, and remote hearings.
- **Ethical Oversight:** Preserves data privacy, accountability, and justice in decisions made with AI assistance.

Impact:

- Speeds up legal proceedings.
- Minimizes human error.
- Enhances impartial, well-informed decision-making.

A hybrid human-AI approach is suggested by emerging trends:

- AI manages extensive research and evidence processing.
- Judges prioritize ethical reasoning, context, and discretion.
- Attorneys use AI insights in their strategic advocacy.

AI transcription and summarizing of proceedings in real time are examples of potential innovations:

- Predictive recommendations for decisions and sentencing guidelines.
- Integrated solutions that combine case administration, contracts, and research into one digital platform.

Particularly in overworked court systems, these developments *offer quicker, more equitable, and more consistent justice.*

Case Study: AI-Powered Family Court Settlement

Pilot initiatives in the UK investigated AI-assisted family dispute mediation:

- Based on past data, legal restrictions, and fairness standards, AI recommended settlement choices.
- Using AI as a decision-support tool, mediators maintained their discretion.
- Participants expressed more satisfaction and quicker resolution times, demonstrating how AI can improve access to justice without taking the place of human judgment.

Diagram: The Digital Bench – Shaping the Future of Justice

Figure 2: The Digital Bench – Shaping the Future of Justice

Conclusion: Moving Toward a Human-Centric Digital Bench

AI is revolutionizing courtrooms through strategic argumentation and evidence analysis. The goal of the digital bench is to enhance human judgment with speed, insight, and data-driven correctness rather than to replace judges or attorneys.

A more general idea that is essential to the future of law is demonstrated by the use of AI in courtrooms:

- Capabilities are enhanced by machines.
- Humans maintain accountability, ethics, and judgment.
- Rather than being outsourced, justice is improved.

In order to ensure that technology innovation is consistent with human rights, justice, and fairness, the following chapter will look at the international ethical and regulatory frameworks governing AI in law.

Chapter 12: Ethics and Regulation: Legal Guidelines for AI

Overview: The Requirement of Governance

Almost every aspect of legal practice has been impacted by artificial intelligence, including contract analysis, predicted judgments, and AI-assisted courtrooms. However, great potential also entails a great deal of responsibility.

The following ethical, legal, and societal issues are brought up by the incorporation of AI into law:

- *How can we guarantee accountability, openness, and fairness in AI-assisted decisions?*
- *When AI recommendations result in harm, who is responsible?*
- *What legal structures can protect human rights and stop prejudice?*

The global ethical and legal frameworks governing AI are examined in this chapter, with an emphasis on norms, principles, and practical applications.

12.1. Fundamental Ethical Precepts

AI in legal contexts is supported by a number of ethical principles:

1. **Fairness**

- AI cannot reinforce or magnify pre-existing prejudices in the judicial system.
- To guarantee that everyone is treated fairly, systems should be inspected on a regular basis.

1. **Transparency**

- Judges, attorneys, and litigants must be able to comprehend and explain decisions or recommendations produced by AI.
- Due process and trust are compromised by black-box algorithms.

1. **Accountability**

- Decisions are ultimately the responsibility of human agents. AI does not make decisions; it is a tool.
- Ethical uncertainty is avoided by clearly assigning blame.

1. **Privacy and Data Protection**:

- Sensitive corporate and personal data is handled by legal AI systems. Effective data governance is crucial.

1. **Human-Centric Design:**

- AI should support human judgment rather than take the place of morality or judgment.

12.2. International Regulatory Structures

AI Act (2024) of the European Union

- AI systems are categorized according to risk, with judicial AI being classified as high-risk.
- Needs human oversight, auditability, and transparency.
- Requires thorough procedures for bias detection and mitigation.

A historic attempt to control AI while striking a balance between innovation and human rights is the AI Act.

AI Principles of the OECD

These principles, which have been embraced by 42 nations, prioritize accountability, human-centered values, and inclusive progress:

- Promotes risk management, auditing, and ongoing AI system monitoring.

UNESCO's 2021 AI Ethics Recommendation

- Promotes human rights, justice, and equity in the application of AI.
- Draws attention to AI's potential to advance fair access to legal services on a worldwide scale.
- Emphasizes the need for human supervision in delicate areas like punishment and conflict settlement.

National Policies

- **United States:** Concentrated on data privacy and bias reduction, especially in sentencing and predictive policing.

- **United Kingdom**: The Law Society's guidelines place a strong emphasis on client confidentiality, transparency, and ethical AI deployment.
- **China:** Uses government instructions to control AI in administrative law and courtrooms, emphasizing uniformity and efficiency.

Although implementation differs by state, these frameworks show a common worldwide commitment to ethically aligned AI.

Case Study: Controlling Artificial Intelligence in Legal Systems

Estonia: Pilot Program for e-Judge:

- AI-assisted preliminary rulings for minor claims are completely auditable.
- Judges retain last say and have the power to reject AI recommendations.
- The system incorporates the ethical values of responsibility, fairness, and transparency.

This paradigm shows how innovation and ethics can coexist, guaranteeing that AI advances justice without compromising human judgment.

12.3. Reducing Discrimination and Bias

Addressing *discrimination and algorithmic prejudice* is one of the most significant ethical issues when implementing Artificial Intelligence (AI) in the legal system. Ensuring fairness, equity, and impartiality becomes both a moral and technical necessity as AI becomes more ingrained in legal research, predictive judgments, and automated decision-making. *If AI's biases are appropriately controlled and reduced, it has the potential to contribute to the creation of a more just and equitable legal system in addition to its speed and accuracy.*

Algorithmic Bias's Origins

AI systems pick up knowledge from data, which frequently *reflects prejudices held by people in the past.* AI can repeat and magnify patterns of unfair treatment based on gender, colour, or socio-economic position seen in previous court rulings, police records, or contract templates. For example, *it has been demonstrated that sentencing algorithms and predictive police systems overstate risk for specific demographic groups, reflecting biases in the training data.*

In the legal sphere, these results jeopardize the fundamental tenet of the EU Charter of Fundamental Rights and the European Convention on Human Rights (ECHR), which is equality before the law.

Explainability and Transparency as Corrective Measures

Transparency, or *the ability to explain and audit AI's decision-making processes,* is the first step towards minimizing **Bias**. All high-risk AI systems, including those employed in law enforcement and justice, are required by the EU AI Act to offer traceable and comprehensible justification for their conclusions. This makes it possible for judges, attorneys, and regulators to spot and contest biased tendencies in data or computational reasoning. *Explainable AI (XAI) solutions restore accountability and supervision by allowing humans to comprehend the reasoning behind a particular decision.*

Diversity of Data and Ethical Education

Diverse, representative, and ethically selected datasets are the first step in reducing **Discrimination**. The entire range of social realities must be included in the inclusive data used to train legal AI. In order to ensure that algorithms represent society's variety rather than its historical disparities, EU initiatives like the European Data Strategy support open, high-quality, and impartial datasets for public-sector AI applications.

Continuous monitoring, bias testing, and ethical auditing all help to guarantee that systems gradually become more equitable.

Human Supervision: The Last Line of Defense

Even the most sophisticated computers are unable to understand social complexity or moral context. Therefore, the best defense against prejudice is still human inspection. Legal technologists, judges, and attorneys must assess AI outputs critically and consider if they are consistent with ethical norms and basic human rights. Humans must maintain control over any decision that impacts rights, freedoms, or dignity, according to the Council of Europe's Ethical Charter on the Use of AI in Judicial Systems.

Developing Algorithmic Justice Trust

The legal community can develop reliable AI systems that not only boost productivity but also promote justice and equality by actively detecting and reducing bias. The objective is to build a responsible ecosystem that continuously learns, audits, and adjusts to preserve the values of impartiality and fairness ingrained in European legislation rather than a flawless algorithm.

AI systems frequently pick up knowledge from past legal data. AI has the potential to reinforce injustices if the data is biased. Diverse training datasets and algorithmic fairness restrictions are two methods to reduce bias:

- Constant assessment and auditing.

- Human supervision for moral and ethical evaluation.

Case Study: Risk Scores for COMPAS

- Racial bias in recidivism forecasts was found through analysis.
- The instrument has to be recalibrated due to ethical oversight, underscoring the necessity of ongoing ethical and regulatory involvement.

In summary, lessening prejudice and discrimination in AI-driven legislation is about more than simply technology; it's about safeguarding the moral basis of justice in general. AI may transform from a mirror of society's historical prejudices into a force for justice, accountability, and inclusive advancement in the digital age through openness, data integrity, and human oversight.

12.4. Responsibility and Liability

The issue of accountability and culpability becomes more crucial as artificial intelligence (AI) plays bigger roles in legal procedures, from contract automation and predictive judgments to digital evidence analysis. Who is responsible for the mistakes or damages caused by an AI system that affects, supports, or even carries out a legal decision on its own? In the European Union (EU), where the commitment to human-centric justice necessitates distinct lines of legal duty, this problem is at the centre of ethical and regulatory discussions.

Shared Accountability in AI-Powered Choices

AI systems are not isolated entities. Complex interactions between developers, deployers, data providers, and end users lead to their decisions. Acknowledging this intricacy, the EU advocates for a shared accountability approach in which all participants in the AI lifecycle are responsible for their respective roles:

- Developers are responsible for making sure the system is visible, safe, and understandable.
- AI must be used properly by employers (such as courts, law firms, or public institutions) while maintaining the proper level of human control.
- Judges, attorneys, and clerks must be aware of the limitations of the system and make sure that its results do not replace human judgment.

Instead of being concealed by opaque technology, this tiered accountability guarantees that mistakes or biases can be tracked, audited, and fixed.

Legal Liability in the Framework of the EU

AI systems, especially those deemed high-risk, will be subject to stringent liability regimes under the upcoming EU AI Liability

Directive and amendments to the Product Liability Directive. This implies that victims will have the right to pursue compensation without having to demonstrate negligence if an AI causes injury (for instance, an incorrect legal suggestion resulting in unjust incarceration or financial loss).

By elucidating how fault and causation apply when judgments are partially or entirely influenced by autonomous systems, the instructions seek to reduce the "accountability gap."

Human Supervision as a Legal Requirement

Human oversight is a legal and moral requirement in court applications. In order to ensure that AI technologies only supplement human reasoning rather than take its place, judges and legal officers must continue to be the final decision-makers. Users of high-risk AI are required by the EU AI Act to comprehend the capabilities, hazards, and operational context of the system. Institutions may be held liable for a breach of duty if such oversight is not provided.

Accountability via Transparency

The foundation of responsible AI deployment is transparency. Legal systems must be traceable, explainable, and documented so that decisions may be examined in retrospect. From data collection to algorithmic output, this documentation establishes a "chain of accountability" that facilitates ethical governance and legal examination. In actuality, this guarantees that accountability is always attributable to a human actor or organization rather than a machine.

Beyond Legal Blame: Ethical Consequences

Additionally, responsibility encompasses ethical obligations in addition to legal culpability. It is the collective moral duty of those who create and implement AI in the legal system to uphold justice, defend fundamental rights, and avoid harm. AI must maintain due process, impartiality, and dignity in addition to adhering to technical requirements.

When legal outcomes are impacted by AI faults, who is at fault?

- **Judges:** Maintain final say over sentencing and decisions.
- **Attorneys:** In charge of making choices based on research or drafting aided by AI.
- **Developers:** Responsible for algorithmic security, transparency, and integrity.
- **Institutions:** Verify the existence of compliance procedures and ethical frameworks.

Public trust is preserved and ethical uncertainty is avoided by clearly defining responsibilities.

In conclusion, maintaining the chain of human accountability in the digital age is the goal of responsibility and liability in AI-driven justice. One fundamental is made quite obvious by the EU's approach: although AI may help administer justice, humans are still responsible for its outcomes. The gavel must always be in human hands in the courtroom of the future, both morally and legally.

12.5. Ethics in Action: AI-Powered Legal Services

The ethical obligations of developers and legal professionals become critical as AI becomes more and more integrated into legal practice. AI-powered legal services are efficient and scalable, but they also present new ethical and professional challenges. These services range from contract assessment and legal research to predictive analytics for case outcomes.

1. **Explainability and Transparency**

   AI systems must give clients and attorneys equally clear reasons for their recommendations. "Black-box" outputs run the danger of eroding responsibility and confidence because the reasoning behind them is unclear. Legal practitioners must be able to defend AI-assisted choices to judges, clients, and regulatory agencies in order to uphold ethical standards.

1. **Professional Responsibility and Accountability**

   Human lawyers are still ultimately in charge, even when AI does analysis or creates contracts. Attorneys must guarantee that AI results are impartial, accurate, and comply with the law. This entails regularly reviewing AI technologies and being ready to reject recommendations as needed.

1. **Preventing Prejudice and Maintaining Equity**

   AI systems may unintentionally reinforce racial, social, or economic prejudices found in their training data. In order to prevent unfair treatment of clients or systemic inequities in legal outcomes, ethical AI in legal services necessitates the proactive identification and mitigation of such biases.

1. **Confidentiality and Privacy**

Privacy issues arise when AI is used to handle sensitive client data. Strict access controls, secure data storage, and strong encryption are requirements for legal AI services. Additionally, attorneys have an ethical obligation to educate their clients about AI's involvement in processing their data.

1. **Knowledgeable Consent**

When AI techniques are utilized in legal proceedings, clients should be properly informed about both the advantages and the drawbacks. To preserve ethics and preserve confidence, informed permission must be obtained.

1. **Constant Observation and Modification**

AI-powered legal services' ethics are dynamic. Lawyers and engineers must constantly assess AI performance, update models, and improve ethical safeguards as laws, social norms, and AI capabilities change.

1. **Example:** AI is currently being used by some legal companies for predictive litigation analytics. Lawyers must use caution when interpreting these projections, let clients know about any uncertainties, and refrain from relying too much on AI forecasts that can affect important legal tactics.

- **Access to Justice**: AI can democratize legal services by giving marginalized groups access to inexpensive research and document drafting.

- **The Risk of Overreliance:** Instead of blindly following machine recommendations, professionals must critically assess AI output.
- **Human Oversight**: In order to perform ethical AI, AI systems must be continuously monitored and validated against social norms and regulatory requirements.

AI in family mediation, for instance, offered reasonable settlement possibilities, but mediators were free to modify them in light of the situation, morality, and context.

It Exhibits the application of ethics without sacrificing human judgment.

In conclusion, merging technological innovation with the fundamental values of legal professionalism—fairness, accountability, and transparency—is the essence of ethics in AI-powered legal services. The legal industry may take use of AI's efficiency while preserving justice and human dignity by incorporating ethical reasoning into its implementation.

12.6. Balancing Ethics and Innovation

A fundamental conflict arises from the quick uptake of AI in legal services: how can the legal industry employ cutting-edge technologies while upholding moral principles? Efficiency, accuracy, and increased access to justice are all promised by innovation, but without rigorous supervision, it runs the risk of eroding public trust, accountability, and fairness. It takes intentional frameworks and procedures to balance these priorities.

1. **Conscientious Innovation**

   Legal AI needs to be both technically sophisticated and morally sound. Anticipating possible risks, carrying out risk analyses, and including precautions from the design stage are all components of responsible innovation. It is the responsibility of both developers and legal experts to make sure AI solutions respect the rule of law and societal norms.

1. **Management of Ethical Risk**

   Risks including bias, mistakes in prediction judgment, or violations of client confidentiality can be introduced by AI systems. Continuous risk monitoring, impact analyses, and systems to mitigate or repair AI-driven errors are necessary to strike a balance between innovation and ethics. Instead than being reactive, ethical oversight ought to be proactive.

1. **Cooperation in Governance**

   It takes multi-stakeholder governance to strike a balance between ethics and innovation, not just lawyers or technologists. To establish guidelines, exchange best practices, and establish limits for the use of AI in legal situations, regulatory organizations, AI developers, legal firms, and civil society must work together.

1. **Including Human Supervision**

Human judgment should never be replaced by innovation. While AI can help with research, writing, and outcome prediction, human oversight is still required for crucial decisions. Ethical principles—justice, fairness, and accountability—remain crucial when human-in-the-loop procedures are maintained.

1. **Openness as a Link**

Transparency promotes trust and facilitates well-informed decision-making. Clients, regulators, and the general public may comprehend AI technology through clear communication about its capabilities, limitations, and decision-making logic. This openness serves as a link between ethical duty and quick innovation.

1. **Ongoing Education and Modification**

Ethics and technology both change throughout time.

In order to adapt to new issues, developing legal precedents, or cultural expectations, lawyers and AI developers must continue to be flexible in upgrading systems, rules, and ethical procedures. A changing ethical framework must coexist with innovation.

Case Example: Take into account AI techniques for predictive litigation. Even while they are highly accurate at predicting case outcomes, depending only on these forecasts without a crucial human evaluation runs the risk of using unfair or biased tactics. AI insights must be used as recommendations rather than deterministic directives in order to strike a balance between innovation and ethics.

Global trends indicate that innovation and regulation are key components of successful AI in law:

1. *Put strong auditing and transparency procedures in place.*
2. *Assure human monitoring in drafting and decision-making.*
3. *Throughout the AI lifecycle, implement bias reduction techniques.*
4. *Comply with human rights, ethical standards, and local legal requirements while deploying AI.*

Regulation guarantees responsible adoption that upholds justice, fairness, and accountability rather than stifling innovation.

Conclusion: The Foundation of Legal AI: Governance

In the era of AI, ethics and regulation are crucial, not optional. *Governing frameworks* make ensuring that human values stay at the forefront of AI's transformation of contract writing, legal research, predictive judgments, and courtrooms.

The future of AI in law will be covered in the upcoming chapter, along with integration, innovation, and the changing role of legal professionals. It will look at how ethics, technology, and human judgment come together to create the justice system of the future.

Thus, the future of the legal industry depends on balancing ethical duty with technological advancement. Law companies may innovate with confidence without sacrificing justice, fairness, or professional integrity by including ethical considerations at every level of AI development and deployment.

Chapter 13: Integration, Innovation, and Human Judgment in the Future of AI in Law

Overview: Moving Towards a New Legal Framework

The question now is not whether AI will change law, but rather how, as it permeates legal research, contract analysis, prediction judgments, and judicial procedures. The integration of AI into the human-centered legal ecosystem—*which combines innovation with ethical monitoring, strategic thinking, and judgment*—holds the key to the future of legal practice.

Using examples from around the world, this chapter examines the new trends, technology integration, and professional development that characterize the coming legal period.

13.1. AI Systems' Convergence in Law

The confluence of several AI systems, each with a focus on a distinct facet of legal practice, is gradually reshaping the legal landscape. These systems no longer function independently, from e-discovery and compliance monitoring to contract automation and predictive analytics. Through its integration, a synergistic ecosystem is created that has the potential to revolutionize the practice, interpretation, and delivery of law.

1. **The Development of a Networked Legal AI Ecosystem**

   AI applications in law have historically been compartmentalized, with one tool used for research, another for contract evaluation, and still another for case prediction. These tools may now cooperate thanks to developments in data standardization, cloud computing, and interoperability. A contract review AI, for example, can provide insights into a predictive litigation tool, resulting in an ongoing feedback loop that increases speed and accuracy.

1. **Advantages of AI Convergence**

   - **Improved Decision-Making:** Attorneys obtain a comprehensive understanding of situations, risks, and contractual duties by integrating outputs from several AI technologies.
   - **Efficiency Gains:** Workflows are streamlined by integrated AI systems, which cut down on effort duplication and speed up legal procedures.
   - **Increased Accuracy:** AI tools' cross-verification reduces errors by identifying discrepancies or missed problems.

- **Predictive Synergy:** By linking past case results, client behaviour, and contractual data, the convergence enables more comprehensive predictive analytics.

1. **Difficulties and Dangers**

Convergence raises issues even when it promises efficiency:

- **Complexity:** Integrated systems may become opaque, making it challenging to follow the logic behind suggestions.
- **Bias Amplification:** Converging AI systems may amplify biases present in underlying datasets across several legal sectors.
- **Accountability:** When several systems interact, it becomes more difficult to assign blame for AI-driven judgments.

1. **Case Example**

Think about a legal practice that handles a lot of business contracts. Potential hazards are identified by a contract analysis AI, and a compliance AI automatically assesses them to determine any regulatory ramifications. Predictive litigation tools evaluate possible conflict outcomes concurrently. This confluence gives attorneys a cohesive, data-driven viewpoint that allows them to make judgments more quickly and intelligently while upholding ethical standards.

1. **Prospects**

Legal practice may develop into a fully integrated, AI-assisted workflow where human attorneys serve as ethical guardians and orchestrators as AI systems continue to converge. The secret will be to strike a balance between intelligence and automation and professional judgment, accountability, and transparency.

AI in law is no longer function-specific. Research, drafting, prediction, and courtroom applications will all be combined into a single platform in future systems:

- **Unified Case Management**: AI continuously monitors contract duties, documents, precedents, and lawsuit risk.
- **Dynamic Legal Research:** Research findings are easily connected to drafting recommendations and forecasting.
- **Automated Compliance Monitoring**: AI regularly looks for changes in regulations and recommends adjustments to contracts and procedures.

Case Study: The Integrated AI Legal Platform in Singapore

AI-assisted research, case management, and decision-support systems are all connected in Singapore's experimental court system. In order to increase efficiency while maintaining human oversight, judges and attorneys engage with a single interface that combines evidence, case law, and risk assessment.

In conclusion, the convergence of AI systems in the legal field signifies a paradigm shift from discrete instruments to interdependent ecosystems. Unprecedented efficiency, predictive insight, and decision assistance are promised by this integration, but it also calls for close consideration of human oversight, ethics, and accountability.

13.2. Human Judgment's Function

Human judgment continues to be the essential cornerstone of justice, notwithstanding the rising sophistication and convergence of AI systems in the legal field. While AI is excellent at processing large amounts of data, spotting trends, and producing predicting insights, it lacks the contextual awareness, ethical judgment, and sophisticated reasoning that only humans can offer. In this way, in AI-assisted legal procedures, human judgment serves as both a guiding and corrective force.

1. **Supervision and Decision-Making Power**

   Although AI can identify hazards, suggest tactics, or forecast case outcomes, attorneys are still ultimately in charge of making decisions. Human judgment guarantees that AI outputs are appropriately evaluated, balanced against legal precepts, and in line with social and ethical standards. As the ultimate arbiters, lawyers verify AI recommendations before putting them into practice.

1. **Interpretation and Contextual Understanding**

   Seldom are legal cases solely based on statistics. Algorithmic analysis frequently misses subtle details, such as the motivations behind a contract clause, the reliability of a witness, or the wider societal ramifications of a decision. The contextual lens that gives AI-generated insights significant importance is provided by human judgment.

1. **Moral and Ethical Argumentation**

AI is unable to independently assess moral issues or find solutions to moral conundrums. In order to ensure that justice is administered in a manner consistent with human values, attorneys incorporate professional ethics, client interests, and social standards into their decision-making. The moral precaution against relying too much on automated forecasts or perhaps skewed results is human judgment.

1. **Error Correction And Risk Management**

Errors, biases, and data restrictions can affect even the most sophisticated AI systems. By examining AI outputs, spotting inconsistencies, and fixing errors before they have an impact on court rulings or client results, human judgment serves as a risk management tool.

1. **Creative and Strategic Thinking**

Innovation, compromise, and flexible problem-solving are frequently needed in legal strategy. AI may make predictions about likely results based on precedent, but human cognitive abilities are necessary to develop creative legal arguments, handle difficult negotiations, or create compelling courtroom tales.

1. **Example:** *Predictive analytics can predict the likelihood that different arguments will be successful in a complicated intellectual property case.* A human attorney, on the other hand, evaluates the opposing party's particular emotional dynamics, ethical issues, and the client's long-term commercial interests. The attorney can create a plan that is both contextually appropriate and data-informed by

combining AI advice with human judgment.

While AI is excellent at speed, scale, and pattern recognition, human judgment is still indispensable:

a. **Contextual Interpretation**: Humans evaluate intent, subtleties, and moral implications; AI can spot patterns.
b. **Ethical Decision-Making**: AI is unable to completely assess fairness, proportionality, and the public interest, which judges and attorneys consider.
c. **Strategic Negotiation:** In contract structure, negotiation, and dispute settlement, human inventiveness and advocacy are still crucial.

Principle: AI is not a substitute for professional knowledge, but rather a co-strategist.

In conclusion, the foundation of AI-enhanced legal practice is human judgment. Even while AI systems offer previously unheard-of analytical capabilities, only people can guarantee that the law is administered in a just, moral, and innovative manner. This complementary relationship, in which human intelligence enhances AI's potential rather than replaces it, is the key to the future of law.

13.3 New Technologies Affecting the Practice of Law

Innovations that are changing established workflows, decision-making procedures, and client involvement are driving a technology revolution in the legal profession. AI is leading the way, but other cutting-edge technologies like blockchain, smart contracts, cloud computing, and legal tech platforms are coming together to completely change the legal profession. To stay competitive and productive, law firms, internal counsel, and legal policymakers must comprehend these technologies.

1. **Machine Learning And Artificial Intelligence (AI)**

Applications of AI in law go well beyond simple automation:

- **Legal Research and Document Review:** AI systems quickly examine vast amounts of statutes, contracts, and case law to find pertinent precedents and irregularities.
- **Predictive Analytics**: AI supports strategic decision-making by forecasting case outcomes, litigation risks, and settlement possibilities.
- **Contract Lifecycle Management**: AI reduces human mistake and speeds up transactions by automating drafting, review, and compliance checks.

1. **Smart Contracts And Blockchain**

Decentralized, unchangeable ledgers made possible by blockchain technology can improve transparency, lower fraud, and expedite transactions. Contractual conditions can be automatically enforced without the need for middlemen thanks to smart contracts, which are blockchain-coded, self-executing agreements. The conventional functions of attorneys in creating, overseeing, and enforcing contracts are being challenged by these technologies.

1. **Legal Tech Platforms And Cloud Computing**

Law companies may centralize data, collaborate remotely, and scale operations effectively with cloud-based solutions. Legal tech platforms reduce administrative costs and allow up attorneys to concentrate on higher-value work by integrating several services, such as document management, e-billing, and case management.

1. **Advanced Analytics and Natural Language Processing (NLP)**

AI systems that comprehend, condense, and draw conclusions from unstructured legal texts are powered by natural language processing (NLP). NLP speeds up ordinary legal work and improves decision accuracy by providing semantic searches, automatic summarization, and intelligent drafting suggestions.

1. **Augmented and Virtual Reality**

Immersion simulations for jury presentations, forensic reconstructions, and trial preparation are made possible by emerging VR/AR technologies. They improve persuasiveness and comprehension by strengthening attorneys' capacity to explain intricate facts and situations.

1. **Data Privacy And Cybersecurity Technologies**

Protecting client data is essential as legal procedures grow more digital. Sensitive data is protected while adhering to data privacy laws thanks to advanced encryption, multi-factor authentication, and AI-driven threat detection systems.

1. **Case Example**: To handle international mergers and acquisitions, a corporate law practice combines cloud collaboration platforms, blockchain-based smart contracts, and AI-powered contract review. Blockchain guarantees enforceable automatic clauses, AI detects possible hazards, and cloud platforms facilitate smooth coordination between multijurisdictional teams. This integration lowers legal exposure while also speeding up the transaction process.

In conclusion, new technologies are catalysts for rethinking the practice of law rather than just instruments. Legal practitioners may improve productivity, accuracy, and client service by utilizing AI, blockchain, NLP, and other advancements. But for integration to be successful, technology adoption must be balanced with moral principles, human judgment, and professional accountability.

13.3. International Case Studies in Integrated AI

Courts, law firms, and regulatory agencies are experimenting with AI-assisted processes globally, demonstrating that the integration of AI into legal institutions is not merely a theoretical endeavour. Examining international case studies highlights the advantages and disadvantages of AI-human cooperation in the legal field, providing important insights for international legal practice.

1. **The US: Contract Analytics and Predictive Litigation**

AI technologies have been used by a number of US courts and law firms for contract administration and predictive litigation analytics. AI is used, for example, by certain corporate legal firms to forecast the probability of case success based on past case data. Lawyers optimize strategy and resource allocation by combining these predictions with human evaluation.

- **Key Takeaway:** Human judgment guarantees moral and strategic choices, whereas predictive analytics increases efficiency but needs to be read contextually.

1. **China: Court Decisions Assisted by AI**

AI techniques are being used more frequently by Chinese courts to evaluate cases and recommend sentences. By autonomously evaluating case papers, forecasting outcomes, and producing draft decisions, the Hangzhou Internet Court pioneered the application of AI for intellectual property and e-commerce conflicts. Judges use AI as a decision-support tool while maintaining final authority.

- **Key Takeaway:** Judges serve as the moral and legal gatekeepers, guaranteeing justice and adherence to the law, while AI improves uniformity and speed in high-volume cases.

1. **Europe: AI in Compliance and Legal Aid**

AI is being employed in Europe, especially in legal aid programs, to increase access to justice. Systems help people navigate administrative processes, complete legal paperwork, and comprehend their rights. AI systems monitor laws in several jurisdictions for corporate compliance, highlighting possible infractions for human examination.

- **Crucial Realization:** AI guarantees regulatory compliance and democratizes access, but accurate interpretation of recommendations requires professional supervision.

1. **Canada: Including AI in Criminal and Family Law**

Initiatives in Canada have investigated the use of AI in criminal and family law to assist in making decisions about bail hearings and custody issues. AI makes suggestions based on past decisions and contextual information that judges and attorneys consider in addition to social, psychological, and ethical considerations.

- **Key Takeaway**: In difficult and delicate situations, integration is most effective when AI enhances human judgment rather than replacing it.

1. **Insights from International Practice**

- **Why Human-in-the-Loop Remains Crucial**: In every jurisdiction, people make the final decisions. AI serves as a supplement, not a replacement.
- **Why Transparency Promotes Trust:** When AI procedures are auditable and explicable, public trust increases.
- **Cross-Border Considerations:** Integrated AI solutions need to take into account variations in regulatory frameworks, legal systems, and cultural norms.
- **Why Bias Mitigation is Crucial:** To stop discriminatory trends from being perpetuated, AI systems educated on past data must be closely watched.

In conclusion, case studies from around the world show that integrating AI into the legal system has revolutionary advantages, including increased access to justice, efficiency, and predictive insight. However, these advantages are only achieved when AI deployment is guided by human oversight, moral judgment, and contextual awareness. Examples from around the world highlight a universal truth: justice is still essentially human, yet technology improves legal practice.

13.4. Legal Lessons from Integrated AI Systems

AI's widespread use in legal practice has offered both encouraging and worrying lessons. Law companies, judges, and legislators can find best practices, foresee obstacles, and create plans for ethical AI integration by looking at foreign case studies. These lessons highlight the need to strike a careful balance between using technology to its full potential and respecting moral and legal norms:

1. **Human Oversight Cannot Be Compromised**

   Maintaining human-in-the-loop procedures is essential for successful AI integration across jurisdictions, including China, Europe, and the United States. As ethical stewards, judges, attorneys, and compliance officials assess AI outputs, apply contextual knowledge, and accept final responsibility for decisions. AI enhances human judgment rather than replaces it.

1. **Explainability and Transparency Develop Trust**

   AI systems must produce results that the public, clients, and legal experts can comprehend. Maintaining trust in AI-assisted legal decisions requires transparent models, audit trails, and explainable reasoning, especially when predictive analytics affect litigation or sentencing.

1. **The Detection And Mitigation Of Bias Are Crucial**

   The data that AI is trained on is reflected in it. If left unchecked, historical biases in contracts, court rulings, and compliance records may spread. To ensure fairness, equity, and justice, effective AI integration necessitates ongoing monitoring, bias testing, and correction processes.

1. **Context Is Important**

The practice of law is highly contextual. International case studies show that AI works best when paired with human judgment that can understand situational, cultural, and social subtleties. Automated analysis and predictive results are recommendations rather than conclusive solutions.

1. **Adoption Is Promoted by Gradual Implementation**

Prior to full-scale integration, law firms and courts can assess AI performance, identify dangers, and improve workflows through pilot programs, staggered rollouts, and selective use cases. Adoption that happens gradually lessens disturbance and boosts legal professionals' trust.

1. **Ethical Standards Must Change as Technology Does**

AI's capabilities require ethical and legal frameworks to change. Accountability, data protection, openness, and the acceptable level of automation should all be covered by policies. Examples from around the world show that proactive ethical oversight keeps the public trust and stops abuse.

1. **Integration is Multidimensional**

Integration is Instead of functioning alone, multi-dimensional AI systems reach their maximum potential when they are integrated across several legal disciplines, such as research, contracts, compliance, and litigation strategy. Although it requires careful coordination and human supervision, synergistic integration increases efficiency, accuracy, and predictive ability.

1. **Case Example:** AI was included for contract analysis, regulatory compliance, and litigation risk assessment by a global firm based in Europe. All AI-generated insights were examined by human attorneys, who also fixed mistakes and contextualized suggestions for regional courts. Faster workflows, lower legal risk, and high stakeholder confidence are the outcomes—a successful model of combining AI and human judgment.

In conclusion, it is evident from the lessons learnt from integrated AI systems that technology enhances legal capacities but does not take the role of human responsibility. Legal professionals may take advantage of AI's transformative potential while preserving justice, fairness, and professional standards by placing a high priority on monitoring, openness, ethical integrity, and contextual judgment.

13.5. Professional and Ethical Requirements

AI integration necessitates adherence to professional and ethical standards:

- **Transparency:** AI's impact on choices must be understood by stakeholders, courts, and clients.
- **Accountability**: People are nevertheless accountable for the results of legal proceedings.
- **Bias Mitigation**: In predictive or analytical AI systems, bias is prevented through ongoing auditing.
- **Ongoing Education**: Lawyers need to stay current on AI literacy, ethics, and regulations.

Only when AI is in line with these requirements can it enhance professional skills.

13.6. The Revolutionary Effect on Legal Professions

AI will change the legal industry in a number of ways:

- **Junior Associates:** Free from monotonous work, concentrating on strategy, analysis, and client interaction.
- **Senior Attorneys:** Enhanced with AI understanding for complicated litigation, high-level judgment, and negotiation.
- **Legal Technologists:** experts that ensure adherence to ethical norms while incorporating AI techniques into practice.

The field will require a hybrid skill set that combines technological proficiency, legal knowledge, and ethical supervision.

13.7. Justice Access and Social Consequences

Legal services will become more accessible thanks to AI:

- *Underprivileged populations save money thanks to automated research and sketching tools.*
- *By guiding dispute settlement, predictive systems reduce backlogs.*
- *In remote or resource-constrained areas, access is increased through AI-assisted mediation and virtual courts.*

However, society must make sure that AI complements human monitoring and rights protections rather than replaces them.

13.8. Future Prospects: Harmonious Human-AI Legal Frameworks

The future of law is increasingly determined by the cooperation of human intelligence and machine capabilities as AI develops and becomes integrated into legal systems across the globe. The most promising path emphasizes synergy—using AI to improve human judgment, efficiency, and access to justice—rather than seeing AI as a replacement for attorneys, courts, or regulators.

1. **The Augmented Lawyer**

AI-assisted workflows will be orchestrated by future lawyers. By fusing AI-powered insights with in-depth legal knowledge, they will:

- Make better strategic choices;
- Pay attention to sophisticated problem-solving, negotiation, and ethical judgment;
- Recognize patterns and threats that are invisible to people alone.

AI will take care of tedious, data-intensive duties, freeing up attorneys to work on high-value projects that call for originality and sophisticated reasoning.

1. **AI Helps Make Decisions, Not Makes Them**

Predictive analytics, contract evaluation, compliance monitoring, and case studies will all continue to be offered via integrated AI systems. However, human oversight is still crucial:

- While AI outputs help make decisions, they are unable to completely comprehend the ethical, cultural, or societal ramifications.
- Human-in-the-loop methods minimize over-reliance on computerized predictions and lessen bias; attorneys and judges ensure that justice is administered fairly and equally.

1. **International Legal Systems and Cross-Border Cooperation**

Cross-border cooperation will grow as legal AI becomes more integrated. AI will be used by international courts and multijurisdictional law firms to deliver worldwide compliance insights, understand various legal codes, and harmonize regulations—all under human supervision.

1. **Regulatory Standards and Ethical AI**

Future advancements will necessitate more robust international norms and ethical frameworks:

- Clear accountability for AI-driven recommendations;
- continuous bias identification and mitigation;
- Transparent AI systems with auditability.

The public's trust in legal institutions will be strengthened rather than weakened by technology advancement thanks to ethical and regulatory control.

1. **Increasing Justice Access**

AI-human synergy presents previously unheard-of chances to increase access to legal services for marginalized communities:

- People without access to attorneys can receive assistance from automated legal aid websites.
- While AI takes care of ordinary duties, lawyers can spend more time to complex and sensitive cases thanks to predictive tools that streamline case management in high-volume courts.

1. Ongoing Education and Modification

Humans and AI will participate in a feedback loop:

- AI systems pick up knowledge from ethical interventions, contextual insights, and human corrections.
- Humans become increasingly adept at deciphering AI outputs, honing tactics and enhancing judgment.

This mutually beneficial evolution guarantees the continued adaptability, accuracy, and ethical foundation of legal practice.

The ultimate goal is a symbiotic system where:

- *Artificial intelligence (AI) speeds up analysis, prediction, and procedural efficiency.*
- *Humans use ethics, judgment, and strategic oversight.*
- *Professional norms and regulations guarantee responsibility, openness, and fairness.*

By utilizing technology without compromising human values, legal practice will be more accurate, resilient, and accessible in this future.

Conclusion: The Law of Tomorrow

The future of law will be cooperative, ethical, and interconnected. AI will empower judges and attorneys, not replace them, by revolutionizing courtroom procedures, research, drafting, and predictive judgment.

This shift will be spearheaded by legal professionals that embrace AI literacy, ethical frameworks, and strategic oversight, creating a justice system that is quicker, more equitable, and accessible to all.

One thing never changes as AI develops: *every algorithm, forecast, and recommendation must be guided by human judgment, ethics, and accountability*. The future of law is a collaboration for justice by algorithm rather than a machine against human story.

Thus, AI-human synergy—*where robots enhance human abilities rather than replace them*—holds the key to the future of law. Legal professionals can embrace the transformative power of AI to improve efficiency, fairness, and access to justice by embracing teamwork, ethical monitoring, and contextual judgment. The law of the future will be a collaborative effort that combines computer intelligence and human knowledge to produce more intelligent and equitable results.

Epilogue: A Human-Centered Future for Justice in the AI Era

From the beginning of digital justice to AI-driven legal research, contract analysis, predictive judgments, AI-assisted courtrooms, and the developing frameworks of ethics, regulation, and professional practice, *this book has followed the development of law in the age of artificial intelligence.*

One thing is clear as we draw to a close: *technology is a tool, not a substitute for human judgment.* AI has the potential to enhance the impartiality, accuracy, and strategic acumen of judges, attorneys, and mediators rather than to replace them.

a. Oversight, Innovation, and Integration

The legal ecosystem of the future will be human-centered, dynamic, and integrated:

- *AI will analyse large databases, find trends, and offer insights.*
- *Ethical frameworks and regulations will guarantee openness, accountability, and equity, preventing bias and safeguarding rights;*
- *Lawyers and judges will interpret, contextualize, and make decisions guided by human ethics and social values.*

The ideal system is *symbiotic,* with *technology and people cooperating* to provide justice more effectively, reliably, and easily.

b. Takeaways from Case Studies

Global examples show that AI may enhance judicial outcomes while maintaining human oversight, from Singapore's integrated platforms to China's Smart Courts, from U.S. predictive analytics to EU ethical monitoring.

These incidents highlight a fundamental fact: *AI flourishes in environments where humans exercise discretion, morality, and accountability.*

Without human oversight, technology runs the risk of making mistakes, becoming biased, and eroding public confidence in the legal system.

c. The Changing Function of Attorneys

Legal occupations will be transformed by AI, not eliminated:

- *Freed from monotonous work, junior attorneys will concentrate on strategy, analysis, and client interaction.*
- *Judges and senior attorneys will use AI insights to make critical decisions.*
- *Legal technologists will make sure AI systems are safe, moral, and compliant with the law.*

In order to properly interpret machine-generated insights, future legal practitioners need to be bilingual in both law and AI literacy.

d. Impact on Society and Access to Justice

Legal services could become more accessible thanks to AI:

- *Underprivileged populations can now access legal aid thanks to reasonably priced research and writing tools.*
- *AI-assisted mediation and predictive analytics can improve dispute resolution and decrease the backlog of cases.*
- *Participation is increased by virtual and hybrid courtrooms, especially in areas with low resources or remote locations.*

However, technology cannot guarantee justice on its own. Human supervision, moral dedication, and social awareness are still crucial.

e. An Outlook for the Future

In the upcoming decades, how humans and robots work together will establish legislation rather than AI taking the place of humans:

- *AI increases capacity for automation, prediction, and data processing.*
- *Humans maintain moral reasoning, strategy, ethics, and justice.*
- *Benefits to society include quicker, more equitable, and more easily accessible legal systems.*

Future laws will be more intelligent, fair, and flexible—but only if people continue to be at the centre of all decisions.

f. Concluding Thoughts

"Justice by Algorithm" is *a call to responsible innovation, not an oxymoron*. AI in law is revolutionary, yet it is constrained by human accountability, ethics, and judgment. The dilemma of utilizing AI's capability without sacrificing our commitment to justice is evident as technology advances.

The adventure is just getting started. *The challenge for judges, attorneys, and society as a whole is not whether AI will alter the law, but rather whether we will use it sensibly, morally, and compassionately.*

In the era of AI, justice is achievable. However, it will be a human-led, machine-assisted justice for humanity.

Table of Figures

Bibliography

1. *Mantelero, Alessandro (2024). "The Fundamental Rights Impact Assessment (FRIA) in the AI Act: Roots, legal obligations and key elements for a model template"*[1]*. Computer Law & Security Review.* ***54*** *106020. arXiv*[2]*:2411.15149*[3]*. doi*[4]*:10.1016/j.clsr.2024.106020*[5]*. ISSN*[6] *0267-3649*[7]*.*

2. *Mantelero, Alessandro (2022), Beyond Data. Human Rights, Ethical and Social Impact Assessment in AI, Information Technology and Law Series, vol. 36, The Hague: Springer-T.M.C. Asser Press, doi*[8]*:10.1007/978-94-6265-531-7*[9]*, ISBN*[10] *978-94-6265-533-1*[11]

3. *Mühlhoff, Rainer; Ruschemeier, Hannah (2024). "Regulating AI with Purpose Limitation for Models"*[12]*. Journal of AI Law and Regulation.* ***1*** *(1): 24–39. doi*[13]*:10.21552/aire/2024/1/5*[14]*.*

1. *https://doi.org/10.1016%2Fj.clsr.2024.106020*
2. *https://en.wikipedia.org/wiki/ArXiv_(identifier)*
3. *https://arxiv.org/abs/2411.15149*
4. *https://en.wikipedia.org/wiki/Doi_(identifier)*
5. *https://doi.org/10.1016%2Fj.clsr.2024.106020*
6. *https://en.wikipedia.org/wiki/ISSN_(identifier)*
7. *https://search.worldcat.org/issn/0267-3649*
8. *https://en.wikipedia.org/wiki/Doi_(identifier)*
9. *https://doi.org/10.1007%2F978-94-6265-531-7*
10. *https://en.wikipedia.org/wiki/ISBN_(identifier)*
11. *https://en.wikipedia.org/wiki/Special:BookSources/978-94-6265-533-1*
12. *https://aire.lexxion.eu/article/AIRE/2024/1/5*
13. *https://en.wikipedia.org/wiki/Doi_(identifier)*
14. *https://doi.org/10.21552%2Faire%2F2024%2F1%2F5*

4. *Veale, Michael; Borgesius, Frederik Zuiderveen (1 August 2021). "Demystifying the Draft EU Artificial Intelligence Act — Analysing the good, the bad, and the unclear elements of the proposed approach". Computer Law Review International.* **22** *(4): 97–112. arXiv[15]:2107.03721[16]. doi[17]:10.9785/cri-2021-220402[18]. ISSN[19] 2194-4164[20]. S2CID[21] 235765823[22].*

5. *Pasick, Adam (March 27, 2023). "Artificial Intelligence Glossary: Neural Networks and Other Terms Explained"[23]. The New York Times. ISSN[24] 0362-4331[25]. Archived[26] from the original on September 1, 2023. Retrieved March, 7, 2025.*

6. *"How Generative AI Can Augment Human Creativity"[27]. Harvard Business Review. June 16, 2023. ISSN[28] 0017-8012[29]. Archived[30] from the original on June 20, 2023. Retrieved March, 7, 2025.*

---

15. *https://en.wikipedia.org/wiki/ArXiv_(identifier)*

16. *https://arxiv.org/abs/2107.03721*

17. *https://en.wikipedia.org/wiki/Doi_(identifier)*

18. *https://doi.org/10.9785%2Fcri-2021-220402*

19. *https://en.wikipedia.org/wiki/ISSN_(identifier)*

20. *https://search.worldcat.org/issn/2194-4164*

21. *https://en.wikipedia.org/wiki/S2CID_(identifier)*

22. *https://api.semanticscholar.org/CorpusID:235765823*

23. *https://www.nytimes.com/article/ai-artificial-intelligence-glossary.html*

24. *https://en.wikipedia.org/wiki/ISSN_(identifier)*

25. *https://search.worldcat.org/issn/0362-4331*

26. *https://web.archive.org/web/20230901183440/https:/www.nytimes.com/article/ai-artificial-intelligence-glossary.html*

27. *https://hbr.org/2023/07/how-generative-ai-can-augment-human-creativity*

28. *https://en.wikipedia.org/wiki/ISSN_(identifier)*

29. *https://search.worldcat.org/issn/0017-8012*

7. *"What is ChatGPT, DALL-E, and generative AI?"*[31]*. McKinsey. Archived*[32] *from the original on April 23, 2023. Retrieved March, 7, 2025.*

---

30. *https://web.archive.org/web/20230620073042/https:/hbr.org/2023/07/how-generative-ai-can-augment-human-creativity*

31. *https://www.mckinsey.com/featured-insights/mckinsey-explainers/what-is-generative-ai*

32. *https://web.archive.org/web/20230423114030/https:/www.mckinsey.com/featured-insights/mckinsey-explainers/what-is-generative-ai*

Don't miss out!

Visit the website below and you can sign up to receive emails whenever Patrick Mukosha publishes a new book. There's no charge and no obligation.

https://books2read.com/r/B-A-HJNZ-XYOZH

Did you love *AI in Law: Justice by Algorithm*? Then you should read *AI in Education: Teaching the Machines to Teach*[33] by Patrick Mukosha!

[34]

AI in Education: Teaching the Machines to Teach

What happens when machines not only assist in learning but begin to *teach*? This ground-breaking book takes readers inside the rapidly evolving world of Artificial Intelligence in education, where algorithms are reshaping how knowledge is delivered, assessed, and personalized.

From classrooms equipped with adaptive tutoring systems to universities experimenting with automated grading and virtual teaching assistants, *AI in Education* reveals both the opportunities and the challenges of this transformation. Rich with real-world examples,

33. https://books2read.com/u/mgO10q

34. https://books2read.com/u/mgO10q

it shows how AI can help close learning gaps, empower students with disabilities, and support teachers in managing ever-growing workloads.

But this is not just a story of technological advancement—it is a human story. The book explores the irreplaceable role of educators as mentors, motivators, and ethical guides in an age when machines can replicate many cognitive tasks but not empathy, creativity, or moral judgment. It raises critical questions about equity, ethics, and the future of work for teachers and learners alike.

Accessible, insightful, and forward-looking, ***AI in Education: Teaching the Machines to Teach*** is an essential read for educators, policymakers, technologists, and parents who want to understand—and help shape—the future of learning in an AI-powered world.

"Where human wisdom meets machine intelligence—the future of teaching begins." – Patrick Mukosha

About the Author

Patrick Mukosha is an ICT & Management Consultant. With 15+ years of IT experience, he's passionate about all things ICT. He also loves to bring ICT down to a level that everyone can understand. His works have been quoted on Academia by Researchers and ICT Practitioners (www.academia.edu). He has a PHD and MBA from AIU, USA, BSc(Hons) ICT, UEA, UK, Dipl, CCT, UK. He's a founder of PatWest Technologies.

www.ingramcontent.com/pod-product-compliance
Lightning Source LLC
LaVergne TN
LVHW090354210926
848480LV00002B/338